35 Special Dangerous Decrees

PRAYER M. MADUEKE

ISBN: 978-1466244108

Published by Prayer Publications.
Printed in the United States of America.

4 Free Ebooks

In order to say a 'Thank You' for purchasing *35 Special Dangerous Decrees*, I offer these books to you in appreciation. Click or type madueke.com/free-gift in your browser.

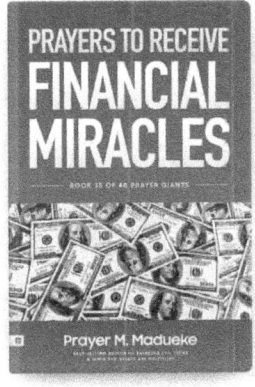

Message from the Author

I want to see you succeed, grow, and break free from negativity and obstacles. My hope is for you to thrive, unaffected by negative influences and challenging situations. Because of that, please permit me to introduce two courses that I believe passionately will help you:

1. To break the evil altars and powers of your father's house, The role of altars in the realm of existence is very key because altars are meeting places between the physical and the spiritual, between the visible and the invisible.

    Unless a man cuts off the evil flow from the power of his father's house, he will not fulfil his destiny. Click here to learn more about my course on how to tear down unholy altars and close the enemy's entryways into your life!

2. To help you seamlessly break iron-like problems, illness, delayed marriage, poverty, or any long-standing battle.

Discover <u>the transformative power of Christian fasting and prayer</u>. Remember, Matthew 17:21 teaches us, *"But this kind of demon does not go out except by prayer and fasting."* Ready to overcome your struggles? <u>Click here</u> to learn more about this course.

Embrace the journey ahead with faith, for through prayer, fasting, and the dismantling of evil altars, you shall unlock the doors to spiritual liberation and divine breakthrough. May your path be illuminated by His grace as you walk towards a life free from bondage.

If you're seeing this from the physical copy, type the link: <u>madueke.com/courses</u> in your browser to view all the courses on my website.

Prayer Madueke
CHRISTIAN AUTHOR

Christian Counselling

We were created for a greater purpose than only survival and God wants us to live a full life.

If you need prayer or counselling, or if you have any other inquiries, please visit the counselling page on my website to know when I will be available for a phone call.

Click or type links.madueke.com/counselling in your browser.

Let's Connect on Youtube ▶

Join me on my YouTube channel, "Prayer M. Madueke," where I share powerful insights, guidance, and prayers for spiritual breakthroughs.

Subscribe today to unlock the secrets of the Kingdom and embrace an abundant life. Let's grow together!

Click or type links.madueke.com/youtube in your browser.

Table of Contents

Dedication

To God Almighty, who has sustained me in His strength and grace. He is so loving and is always by my side.

Acknowledgment

I would like to acknowledge the immeasurable and unquantifiable encouragement of Dr. Daniel Olukoya, general overseer, Mountain of Fire and Miracles Ministries, who has supported me spiritually in my ministry. Without his vision, this book would not have seen the light of the day.

And my lovely wife, Roseline C. Madueke, whose divine sacrifices have been my motivation.

CHAPTER ONE

Evil Decrees

When we speak of decree, we mean a strong and unshakeable utterance, or exercise of power through word and command, which is next to certainty. A decree can also be in form of an order that has equivalent force of law. It can be defined also as a religious ordinance enacted by a council or a particular head.

A decree is a way of foreordaining wills. It is like a judgment delivered in a probate court, which confirms an order judicially. Decrees take many forms. There are good decrees, as well as bad and evil decrees. While an evil decree can bring someone under the influence of curses, spells and all manner of evil, good decrees, sometimes rendered forcefully, set people free and brings restoration and serenity.

When an evil person says any evil thing and stands firm on it, those words actually become evil decree. An evil decree can destroy or kill. Evil decrees cannot be taken to be simple evil wishes against people; rather they are strong evil utterances or commands said in forceful manners. Evil decrees are evil words put together to torment peoples' lives.

They bring invisible barriers that can keep people out of God's programs and promises. Evil decrees frustrate everything their victims do and can bring frustration at the verge of success. It is a decree said to limit a person or persons to certain levels of life. Evil decrees can cause many problems in peoples' lives. They put people under serious bondages. Evil decrees can cause premature deaths. Evil decrees cause fatal accidents, losses of lives and destroy marriages. An evil decree can bring someone under the power of poverty. An evil decree can stimulate someone to commit suicide and can make people marry at later ages of their lives. Yokes of mental illness can be imposed on people through evil decrees.

Evil decrees initiate uncontrollable desires for immorality. It brings spiritual blindness and makes people to siphon off treasuries. When one is under the influence of evil decree, such a person would not see things rightly. He or she would likely come under the control of errors, taking actions one is not supposed to take. It can also bring depression and feelings of dejection.

It could make people to be unreasonably harsh and unteachable. It can cause people to come under the yoke of vagabond spirits. Victims of evil decrees can be manipulated easily. Evil decrees bring all sorts of things that lead to spiritual backwardness. That is why a brilliant student could suddenly become a dullard and begin to fail exams. Evil decrees can bring people under periodical failures. They put people under demonic powers. That is exactly when people become confused in life, suffering from incurable diseases. Evil decrees facilitate sudden disappearance of good things. They can cause a very rich person to become a beggar and remain under an evil mark. Evil decrees pollute peoples' characters.

It is possible for someone under the influence of an evil decree to be deformed in life. In such cases, such people's destinies are buried while they still live. Dangerous decrees can cause you to lose your job in mysteriously circumstances and prevent you from getting other jobs. It can place people under the yoke of barrenness for years and if such evil decrees are not revoked, such victims would stay barren the rest of their lives.

Evil decrees subject people to pains, agony and prolonged sufferings. They cause miscarriages and painful menstruation. Dangerous decrees can shut the doors of true riches. Evil decrees are often the root of extreme hatred and unavoidable divorces. When a child is under the influence of dangerous decree, such a child's behaviors would be strange.

A Christian under the influence of evil decrees cannot enjoy good things for a long time. Such Christians will continue to experience incessant setbacks in every endeavor. This is because evil decrees cause people to fail in all their ventures. People under this influence are hindered to receive true miracles of God. Instead, they remain entangled with wrong people in life, who influence them to make costly mistakes that can their lives. An evil decree can cause destruction in a twinkle of an eye. It can make an industrious or busy person to become lazy and unprofitable suddenly. Evil decrees multiply sorrow, worry and anxiety.

CHAPTER TWO

Dangerous Decrees

When Nebuchadnezzar became the king of Babylon, he had a terrible dream in the second year of his reign. His spirit was troubled greatly for he could not tell the meaning of his dream. As a result, sleep departed from him. Therefore, he summoned all the magicians, astrologers, and sorcerers in his entire Kingdom. In fact, the whole situation was so complicated because Nebuchadnezzar had forgotten his dream. Therefore, he charged all the magicians, astrologers and sorcerers to make known to him his dreams and their interpretations, and threatened to pass a decree to cut them to pieces and their houses made a dunghill (Daniel 2:5-9).

Dangerous decrees are normally made under the influence of evil spirits of anger. Dangerous decrees can be made against an individual, group, or even a whole nation. So, in anger the king commanded that the wise men of Babylon should be destroyed, and he furiously made a decree to that effect. The only condition for the wise men to live was to make the dream and its interpretation known to the king, or they face the wrath of the decree.

"For this cause the king was angry and very furious, and commanded to destroy all the wise men of Babylon. And the decree went forth that the wise men should be slain; and they sought Daniel and his fellows to be slain. Then Daniel answered with counsel and wisdom to Arioch the captain of the king's guard, which was gone forth to slay the wise men of Babylon: He answered and said to Arioch the king's captain, why is the decree so hasty from the king? Then Arioch made the thing known to Daniel" (Daniel 2:12-15).

Note that the decree did not affect the righteous only, but all the wise men in Babylon and the unrighteous. Daniel and his group of righteous men would be affected obviously. Dangerous decrees, once passed, can affect both the good and the bad. That is why when a dangerous decree is issued against any family, whether in the past or present, there is an urgency to revoke it. Evil decrees do not know whether you are born again or not.

As a born again, you then have to do something to reverse or counter such evil decrees. Otherwise, you would be affected just like every other person. If Nebuchadnezzar's decree could affect righteous people like Daniel and the three Hebrew children, then it is possible that evil decrees could affect us as well. Likewise, many great people of God have died for neglecting to deal with evil decrees issued against their ancestors or against them. It is time for you to rise up and revoke all dangerous evil decrees said against your life and families in the past or present.

"And the decree went forth that the wise men should be slain; and they sought Daniel and his

fellows to be slain. Then Daniel answered with counsel and wisdom to Arioch the captain of the king's guard, which was gone forth to slay the wise men of Babylon: He answered and said to Arioch the king's captain, Why is the decree so hasty from the king? Then Arioch made the thing known to Daniel. Then Daniel went in, and desired of the king that he would give him time, and that he would shew the king the interpretation. Then Daniel went to his house, and made the thing known to Hananiah, Mishael, and Azariah, his companions: That they would desire mercies of the God of heaven concerning this secret; that Daniel and his fellows should not perish with the rest of the wise men of Babylon. Then was the secret revealed unto Daniel in a night vision. Then Daniel blessed the God of heaven" (Daniel 2:13-19).

When a Christian revokes dangerous decrees against his life, he or she progresses and enjoys promotions. Impossible things would become possible and yokes would be broken. But if you are not born again, there is a limit your occultism can go to protect you. But for our God, He knows everything and has all the power to change all situations.

That is why when Daniel and his men started praying for revelation on what to do, God intervened and made an impossible thing possible.

"Daniel answered in the presence of the king, and said, The secret which the king hath demanded cannot the wise men, the astrologers, the magicians, the soothsayers, shew unto the king; But there is a God in heaven that revealeth secrets, and maketh known to the king Nebuchadnezzar what shall be in the latter days. Thy dream, and the visions of thy head upon thy bed, are these... Thou sawest till that a stone was cut out without hands, which smote the image upon his feet that were of iron and clay, and brake them to pieces. Then was the iron, the clay, the brass, the silver, and the gold, broken to pieces together, and became like the chaff of the summer threshing floors; and the wind carried them away, that no place was found for them: and the stone that smote the image became a great mountain, and

filled the whole earth. This is the dream; and we will tell the interpretation thereof before the king. Thou, O king, art a king of kings: for the God of heaven hath given thee a kingdom, power, and strength, and glory. And wheresoever the children of men dwell, the beasts of the field and the fowls of the heaven hath he given into thine hand, and hath made thee ruler over them all. Thou art this head of gold. And after thee shall arise another kingdom inferior to thee, and another third kingdom of brass, which shall bear rule over all the earth. And the fourth kingdom shall be strong as iron: forasmuch as iron breaketh in pieces and subdueth all things: and as iron that breaketh all these, shall it break in pieces and bruise. And whereas thou sawest the feet and toes, part of potters' clay, and part of iron, the kingdom shall be divided; but there shall be in it of the strength of the iron, forasmuch as thou sawest the iron mixed with miry clay. And as the toes of the feet were part of iron, and part of clay, so the kingdom shall be partly strong, and partly broken. And whereas thou sawest iron mixed with miry clay, they shall mingle themselves with the seed of men: but they shall not cleave one to another, even as iron is not mixed with clay. And in the days of these kings shall the God of heaven set up a kingdom, which shall never be destroyed: and the kingdom shall not be left to other people, but it shall break in pieces and consume all these kingdoms, and it shall stand for ever. Forasmuch as thou sawest that the stone was cut out of the mountain without hands, and that it brake in pieces the iron, the brass, the clay, the silver, and the gold; the great God hath made known to the king what shall come to pass hereafter: and the dream is certain, and the interpretation thereof sure" (Daniel 2:27-28, 34-45).

However, Nebuchadnezzar was so touched, after Daniel's interpretation that he humbled himself and fell upon his face, and for the first time in the history of Babylon, their king worshipped Daniel's God and belittled his own gods. That single act of the king brought into Daniels' life good things and made him a great person above ordinary man. He was also promoted above all his equals and his friends received promotions in Babylon.

"Then the king Nebuchadnezzar fell upon his face, and worshipped Daniel, and commanded that they should offer an oblation and sweet odors unto him. The king answered unto Daniel, and said, of a truth it is, that your God is a God of gods, and a Lord of kings, and a revealer of secrets, seeing thou couldest reveal this secret. Then the king made Daniel a great man, and gave him many great gifts, and made him ruler over the whole province of Babylon and chief of the governors over all the wise men of Babylon. Then Daniel requested of the king, and he set Shadrach, Meshach, and Abed-nego, over the affairs of the province of Babylon: but Daniel sat in the gate of the king" (Daniel 2:46-49).

Dangerous decrees can be issued against you directly or indirectly. It can be inherited too. But what is important is that whichever way it comes, they need to be revoked before irreversible damages are done. King Nebuchadnezzar backslide and became very satanic to the extent that his words became equivalent to Satan's decrees.

Once he opened his mouth to say anything, his words were taken as decrees that cannot be reversed. Disobeying his words, whether for good or bad reasons, attracted death penalty.

In one of his foolish statements, his speech affected God and his people. He made an idol of gold and commanded that all the people in his kingdom must bow down and worship that particular idol, including God's children (Daniel 3:6). It was after that decree that some wicked people found out that the three Hebrew children were not obeying the king's decree at the expense of their God; God of Abraham, Isaac and Jacob. Thus, they were accused and condemned to die.

"Thou, O king, hast made a decree, that every man that shall hear the sound of the cornet, flute, harp, sackbut, psaltery, and dulcimer, and all kinds of musick, shall fall down and worship the golden image: And whoso falleth not down and worshippeth, that he should be cast into the midst of a burning fiery furnace. There are certain Jews

whom thou hast set over the affairs of the province of Babylon, Shadrach, Meshach, and Abed-nego; these men, O king, have not regarded thee: they serve not thy gods, nor worship the golden image which thou hast set up" (Daniel 3:10-12).

Therefore, you must be ready to fight or revoke dangerous decrees, if you want to successfully live in any territory, without following after evil decrees or satanic sanctions associated with such territories. If you desire a successful marriage without marital failures, you must be ready to revoke dangerous decrees affecting marriages in your family.

Equally, dangerous decrees are responsible for evil occurrences in family lineages. As a believer, you must rise up at once against evil decrees, otherwise you may end up badly, even as a true Christian. This can also explain why so many Christians are poor, wretched, sick and defeated in life. The ultimate purpose of Satan is to bring people of the nations under evil decrees and mess up their lives.

Is it not convincing how the courage of three young Hebrew children forced Nebuchadnezzar to retract his evil decrees with his own mouth? Whenever evil decrees are revoked, believers get freed and promoted.

> *"Therefore I make a decree, That every people, nation, and language, which speak anything amiss against the God of Shadrach, Meshach, and Abed-nego, shall be cut in pieces, and their houses shall be made a dunghill: because there is no other God that can deliver after this sort. Then the king promoted Shadrach, Meshach, and Abed-nego, in the province of Babylon" (Daniel 3:29-30).*

One of the worst things that can happen to a true believer is for a believer to be ignorant of evil and dangerous decrees prevailing over his or her life. Unfortunately, many Holy Ghost filled Christians do not believe that there are evil decrees affecting them, especially when they are under the manipulation of witchcraft powers. Evil people are constantly passing decrees every now and then on earth, while leaders, kings and presidents of many nations are continuously entering into covenants with many dangerous spirits.

These distasteful acts are affecting the lives of so many Christians all over the world. These are wicked personalities, who decree daily in attempt to paralyze the program of God's people. If gifted people, like Daniel, are not around to interpret certain things, lives of many true believers would be wasted easily by evil decrees.

"Therefore made I a decree to bring in all the wise men of Babylon before me, that they might make known unto me the interpretation of the dream... This matter is by the decree of the watchers, and the demand by the word of the holy ones: to the intent that the living may know that the most High ruleth in the kingdom of men, and giveth it to whomsoever he will, and setteth up over it the basest of men... This is the interpretation, O king,

and this is the decree of the most High, which is come upon my lord the king" (Daniel 4:6, 17, 24).

On many occasions, decrees that would have ended Daniel's life were issued. But he did not keep quiet like many believers are doing today. Believers can no longer afford to watch silently as unbelievers say, whatever they wanted without being challenged. If Daniel had kept quiet and allowed unbelievers to say things without being challenged, his life would have been a mess.

"All the presidents of the kingdom, the governors, and the princes, the counselors, and the captains, have consulted together to establish a royal statute, and to make a firm decree, that whosoever shall ask a petition of any God or man for thirty days, save of thee, O king, he shall be cast into the den of lions. Now, O king, establish the decree, and sign the writing, that it be not changed, according to the law of the Medes and Persians, which altereth not. Wherefore king Darius signed the writing and the decree" (Daniel 6:7-9).

Satanic agents and spirit beings are monitoring with ease people that would not decree dangerous decrees. They keep vigils in order to watch and report people who are aspiring to escape evil chains, tied upon them through evil decrees. Such evil personalities and spirit beings are not happy when they see true Christians under such decrees prosper. They report such persons to appropriate evil quarters for punishment. That is why you see many Christians rising and falling daily. Whenever they are about to become successful, evil agents employ all available weapons to attack and pull them down. They also monitor people's lives and progresses in marriage.

"Then they came near, and spake before the king concerning the king's decree; Hast thou not signed a decree, that every man that shall ask a petition of any God or man within thirty days, save of thee, O king, shall be cast into the den of lions? The king answered and said, the thing is true, according to the law of the Medes and Persians, which altereth not. Then answered they and said before the king,

That Daniel, which is of the children of the captivity of Judah, regardeth not thee, O king, nor the decree that thou hast signed, but maketh his petition three times a day. Then the king, when he heard these words, was sore displeased with himself, and set his heart on Daniel to deliver him: and he labored till the going down of the sun to deliver him. Then these men assembled unto the king, and said unto the king, Know, O king, that the law of the Medes and Persians is, that no decree or statute which the king establisheth may be changed" (Daniel 6:12-15).

That is why it is so hard for believers to occupy certain offices, like offices of the president, governors, members of parliament, directors, etc. Big contracts, projects and high positions in governments are out of reach for many believers because of evil decrees placed upon their lives. Instead, such government contracts are assigned only to men who are in the occult. Such men can do whatever that is necessary to terminate the life of people who defile their occult ranks or group.

"Then the king commanded, and they brought Daniel, and cast him into the den of lions. Now the king spake and said unto Daniel, Thy God whom thou servest continually, he will deliver thee. And a stone was brought and laid upon the mouth of the den; and the king sealed it with his own signet, and with the signet of his lords; that the purpose might not be changed concerning Daniel" (Daniel 6:16-17).

Everyday, evil decrees are issued against Christians all over the world. Your business, life, finance, health, breakthroughs, etc., could be stunted because of being locked up in lion's den. Your certificate may be locked up in lion's den through a dangerous decree. If any part of your life is locked up in lions' den through a dangerous decree, you may not succeed in life except you start fighting your battle early. When you begin revoking all wicked decrees made upon your life courageously, you will begin to experience God's favor.

"Then king Darius wrote unto all people, nations, and languages, that dwell in all the earth; Peace be multiplied unto you. I make a decree, that in every dominion of my kingdom men tremble and fear before the God of Daniel: for he is the living God, and steadfast forever, and his kingdom that which shall not be destroyed, and his dominion shall be even unto the end. He delivereth and rescueth, and he worketh signs and wonders in heaven and in earth, who hath delivered Daniel from the power of the lions. So this Daniel prospered in the reign of Darius and in the reign of Cyrus the Persian" (Daniel 6:25-28).

The Bible made it very clear that dangerous decrees are not to be allowed to affect God's people. When we confront evil decrees before their manifestation, then our deliverances will appear suddenly.

"In the day that thy walls are to be built, in that day shall the decree be far removed" (Micah 7:11).

CHAPTER THREE

Decrees of Evil Men of Our Time

"Woe unto them that decree unrighteous decrees, and that write grievousness which they have prescribed; To turn aside the needy from judgment, and to take away the right from the poor of my people, that widows may be their prey, and that they may rob the fatherless! And what will ye do in the day of visitation, and in the desolation which shall come from far? to whom will ye flee for help? and where will ye leave your glory?" (Isaiah 10:1-3).

One of the most absurd stories I have ever heard was about a very rich man in Africa. He was said to be richer than even his own country. His businesses spanned across the continents of the world. Shortly before he became so rich, it was said that he engaged some mallams and ritualists in a business of evil decreeing. One of his employed mallams has to travel to the middle of the sea with a flying boat every 2:00am. He was to perform a sacrifice, accompanied with evil and dangerous decrees, at the centre of the sea. No one alive is expected to know, even the mallams' families. The mallams have to travel in small groups. Their job was to offer a ram at midnights and make incantations of decrees till morning.

While other mallams chanted, the senior mallam carried out sacrifices at the centre of the sea. There, he was expected to have a direct contact with marine powers. These sacrifices went on for 180 days, and afterwards, that particular man became extremely rich. In fact, he became a small god and grand master of the occult. He rose above all mallams, who were his masters earlier. His words became decrees. He employed so many experts, who decreed day and night and communicated with demons on his behalf.

Story has it that recently, he imported a group of mallams from another country to decree certain things for him. Then these mallams were locked up in a particular place. They were not expected to come out of the house for forty days. They made a suicidal vow never to see the sun, moon or stars for those forty days and nights. So they were locked up so they would not to see or talk to any human until the appointed time. However, it was agreed that the day they would come out, under the anointing of devil, they would immediately address the moon, sun, stars and other elementary powers. And so, these foreign mallams went into the underworld with full assurance that once they come out, they would decree anything and it would happen.

Well, that was their faith. But their faith was evil and was intended for evil purposes. But the truth is that if they locked in to what they believed, it would definitely work for them. Evil people go to the extremes when it comes to paying high prices for what they wanted. How could believers not be ready to pay the price of confronting these evil decrees too? In fact, believers, who cannot pay required prices in passing decrees to confront evil decrees, are bound to live under the decree of evil people.

"And when the king of Moab saw that the battle was too sore for him, he took with him seven hundred men that drew swords, to break through even unto the king of Edom: but they could not. Then he took his eldest son that should have reigned in his stead, and offered him for a burnt offering upon the wall. And there was great indignation against Israel: and they departed from him, and returned to their own land" (2 Kings 3:26-27).

In the above reference, there was a war between the Moabites and the children of the Israelites. So, the children of Israel defeated the Moabites and they fled. The children of Israel pursued after them into their own country and burnt down their cities. They destroyed every good piece of land, closed all the wells of water and felled all good trees. In Kirkaraseth, the slingers went about and smote with stones.

Even in the midst of all these, the Moabites refused to give up. They kept on fighting. But when the king of Moab saw that the battle would be lost completely, he took seven hundred men that drew swords to break through but he could not. Thereafter, he took his eldest son that would reign in his stead and offered him for a burnt offering. They stood their grounds and made some dangerous decrees with the blood of the young man. On Israel's side, none was willing to rise up to the challenge and revoke those evil dangerous decrees made with blood, and God was disappointed. The original purpose of God was to deal with the Moabites, but the children of Israel were not ready to confront their evil decrees.

"And Mesha king of Moab was a sheep master, and rendered unto the king of Israel an hundred thousand lambs, and an hundred thousand rams, with the wool. But it came to pass, when Ahab was dead, that the king of Moab rebelled against the

king of Israel. And king Jehoram went out of Samaria the same time, and numbered all Israel. And he went and sent to Jehoshaphat the king of Judah, saying, the king of Moab hath rebelled against me: wilt thou go with me against Moab to battle? And he said I will go up: I am as thou art, my people as thy people, and my horses as thy horses. And he said, which way shall we go up? And he answered, the way through the wilderness of Edom. So the king of Israel went, and the king of Judah, and the king of Edom: and they fetched a compass of seven days' journey: and there was no water for the host, and for the cattle that followed them. And the king of Israel said, Alas! That the LORD hath called these three kings together, to deliver them into the hand of Moab! But Jehoshaphat said, is there not here a prophet of the LORD that we may inquire of the LORD by him? And one of the kings of Israel's servants answered and said, here is Elisha the son of Shaphat, which poured water on the hands of Elijah. And Jehoshaphat said, the word of the LORD is with him. So the king of Israel and Jehoshaphat and the king of Edom went down to him. And Elisha said unto the king of Israel, What have I to do with thee? Get thee to the prophets of thy father, and to the prophets of thy mother. And the king of Israel said unto him, nay: for the LORD hath called these three kings together, to deliver them into the hand of Moab. And Elisha said, As the LORD of hosts liveth, before whom I stand, surely, were it not that I regard the presence of Jehoshaphat the king of Judah; I would not look toward thee, nor see thee. But now bring me a minstrel. And it came to pass, when the minstrel played, that the hand of the LORD came upon him. And he said, thus saith the LORD, Make this valley full of ditches. For thus saith the LORD, Ye shall not see wind, neither shall ye see rain; yet that valley shall be filled with water, that ye may drink, both ye, and your cattle, and your beasts. And this is but a light thing in the sight of the LORD: he will deliver the Moabites also into your hand. And ye shall smite every fenced city, and every choice city, and shall fell every good tree, and stop all wells of water, and mar every good piece of land with stones. And it came to pass in the morning, when the meat offering was offered, that, behold, there came water by the way of Edom, and the country was filled with water" (2 Kings 3:4-20).

Evil decrees of Moabites, together with the blood of their king's son, brought great indignation against Israel and they could not continue with the battle. They departed and returned to their own land.

"And when the king of Moab saw that the battle was too sore for him, he took with him seven hundred men that drew swords, to break through even unto the king of Edom: but they could not. Then he took his eldest son that should have reigned in his stead, and offered him for a burnt offering upon the wall. And there was great indignation against Israel: and they departed from him, and returned to their own land" (2 Kings 3:26-27).

The world is filled with dangerous decrees, whether you believe it or not, and most of these decrees affect believers greatly. Unfortunately, those believers are not fighting back to save their situations.

"Then were the king's scribes called on the thirteenth day of the first month, and there was written according to all that Haman had commanded unto the king's lieutenants, and to the governors that were over every province, and to the rulers of every people of every province according to the writing thereof, and to every people after their language; in the name of king Ahasuerus was it written, and sealed with the king's ring. And the letters were sent by posts into all the king's provinces, to destroy, to kill, and to cause to perish, all Jews, both young and old, little children and women, in one day, even upon the thirteenth day of the twelfth month, which is the month Adar, and to take the spoil of them for a prey. The copy of the writing for a commandment to be given in every province was published unto all people, that they should be ready against that day. The posts went out, being hastened by the king's commandment, and the decree was given in Shushan the palace.

And the king and Haman sat down to drink; but the city Shushan was perplexed" (Esther 3:12-15).

During the time of Esther, a dangerous decree was issued to arrest all the Jews in all the provinces and have them destroyed, both young and old, women and their babies, all in one day. But when Mordecai perceived the imminent peril, he swung into immediate actions. He sent a copy of the decree to Esther to act upon it. Esther was a woman of action, who joined Mordecai in revoking that evil decree.

"When Mordecai perceived all that was done, Mordecai rent his clothes, and put on sackcloth with ashes, and went out into the midst of the city, and cried with a loud and a bitter cry; And came even before the king's gate: for none might enter into the king's gate clothed with sackcloth. And in every province, whithersoever the king's commandment and his decree came, there was great mourning among the Jews, and fasting, and weeping, and wailing; and many lay in sackcloth and ashes. Also he gave him the copy of the writing of

the decree that was given at Shushan to destroy them, to shew it unto Esther, and to declare it unto her, and to charge her that she should go in unto the king, to make supplication unto him, and to make request before him for her people. Then Esther bade them return Mordecai this answer, Go, gather together all the Jews that are present in Shushan, and fast ye for me, and neither eat nor drink three days, night or day: I also and my maidens will fast likewise; and so will I go in unto the king, which is not according to the law: and if I perish, I perish. So Mordecai went his way, and did according to all that Esther had commanded him" (Esther 4:1-3, 8, 15-17).

The result of their prayers was that the decree backfired, all the Jews were spared, and evil plotters were punished. When decrees are revoked, freedom takes its rightful place. Dangerous decrees cannot stand against true children of God, who know how to revoke evil decrees.

"On that night could not the king sleep, and he commanded to bring the book of records of the chronicles; and they were read before the king. And the king said, what honor and dignity hath been done to Mordecai for this? Then said the king's servants that ministered unto him, There is nothing done for him. Let the royal apparel be brought which the king useth to wear, and the horse that the king rideth upon, and the crown royal which is set upon his head: Then took Haman the apparel and the horse, and arrayed Mordecai, and brought him on horseback through the street of the city, and proclaimed before him, Thus shall it be done unto the man whom the king delighteth to honor. And Mordecai came again to the king's gate. But Haman hasted to his house mourning, and having his head covered" (Esther 6:1, 3, 8-12).

Sometime ago when I visited London, I read a daily mail newspaper of Thursday, November 18, 2010, page 62. An article about one Cassandra Eason, one of the world's most famous white witches, shocked me. It is unbelievable that this woman has written dozens of books, including her complete book of spells, which has been translated into 14 languages. In her own words, she said, "I am a modern cyber witch, so I can do online spells or on the phone or do it face to face. I do all sorts of spells, from helping people find love and get pregnant, getting more money and a new job. With most spells I will summon up powers of the earth, water air and fire by doing a small ceremony in my kitchen, using stones or herbs and chanting and dancing." This is incredible and ridiculous. A modern cyber witch? And boasting about it? God forbid!

CHAPTER FOUR

Believer's Decree

God is a God of decree and those who believe in Him are also given the power to decree and it comes to pass. All creatures came into existence because God decreed for them. The heavens, angels, sun, moon, stars and light also came into being because of God's decree. The waters, which are under and above the earth, all came because of God's decree.

> "Praise ye him, all his angels: praise ye him, all his hosts. Praise ye him, sun and moon: praise him, all ye stars of light. He hath also established them forever and ever: he hath made a decree which shall not pass" (Psalms 148:2-3, 6).

Those who pass decrees are imitators of God. Even the wicked imitate God. The Lord God of heaven is the initiator of decrees. Satan uses the advantage of his knowledge over men to teach his agents how to pass decrees against God's people. Decree is a tool meant for God and His children. As the crown of God creation, we have the right to command the elements and elemental powers to obey us. We have the authority, as invested by God, to talk to the moon, sun, stars, and expect them to obey us. The enemies of God are using what rightly belongs to us to fight against us. Believers can decree like God. They can make a decree and it stands. Even ordinary kings of the world, by the virtue of their positions, can also make decrees and God honors them.

"By me king's reign, and princes decree justice. When he gave to the sea his decree, that the waters should not pass his commandment: when he appointed the foundations of the earth" (Proverbs 8:15, 29).

When God passes a decree, it is perpetual, and so it ought to be with true believers. As a believer, when you stand on God's Word and decree a thing, it shall surely stand. No matter the situation, when a true Christian comes out in faith and decrees a thing, it shall stand. The winds might be in the opposite direction at the point of decree. Even circumstances may appear to disagree with you at the point of the decree but they cannot prevail for too long. Enemies may roar, revolt and take their stands but they shall not prevail.

"Fear ye not me? saith the LORD: will ye not tremble at my presence, which have placed the sand for the bound of the sea by a perpetual decree, that it cannot pass it: and though the waves thereof toss themselves, yet can they not prevail; though they roar, yet can they not pass over it?" (Jeremiah 5:22).

Those who know their God very well would know that when God is involved in a decree, nobody can reverse it or prevail over it. Even occult people, who are wise, understand this very well.

"Gather yourselves together, yea, gather together, O nation not desired; Before the decree bring forth, before the day pass as the chaff, before the fierce anger of the LORD come upon you, before the day of the LORD's anger come upon you" (Zephaniah 2:1-2).

"For though thy people Israel be as the sand of the sea, yet a remnant of them shall return: the consumption decreed shall overflow with righteousness" (Isaiah 10:22).

Whenever God is involved in any decree, enemies have no other option than to bow. Joshua once stopped the sun and the moon. It happened before and it can still happen again. Believers have express command from God to decree any thing and expect them to be established. A truly knowledgeable, holy and militant child of God does not fear any situation. That is because God has given believers the power to decree anything we desire.

"Thou shalt also decree a thing, and it shall be established unto thee: and the light shall shine upon thy ways"(Job 22:28).

When you decree a thing or revoke an evil decree against you, light will shine on your ways. And when the light comes, darkness disappears. When a true child of God engages himself in a spiritual exercise like fasting or even ordinary prayers of warfare, anything he or she decrees cannot be challenged by any power.

"To confirm these days of Purim in their times appointed, according as Mordecai the Jew and Esther the queen had enjoined them, and as they had decreed for themselves and for their seed, the matters of the fasting and their cry. And the decree of Esther confirmed these matters of Purim; and it was written in the book" (Esther 9:31-32).

CHAPTER FIVE

The Decree of Faith

Right from the beginning of time, we saw faith in action. God only made declarations, and things came into being. Why was it so? Because God knew that whatever He said would be. That is what is called faith. It is an evidence of saying something and believing it. Believers in the past who obtained good reports got them by faith. To achieve any meaningful thing in life, you must have faith in the word of mouth. You may need to know that wicked people, who believe in their words, also succeed. That is why when two people, who are opposing each other, speak, one must bow to the other. Those who are on the side of God always win all battles.

"For by it the elders obtained a good report. Through faith we understand that the worlds were framed by the word of God, so that things which are seen were not made of things which do appear" *(Hebrews 11:2-3).*

Do not stop talking when there is something to say. Do not stop believing when there are words you have spoken, regardless of prevailing frightful circumstances. As a Christian, you must come out and say something. Believe in what you have said without doubting. Do not stop believing as long as what you have said has not manifested, even to the point of death.

Moses prayed a prayer before he died, but God refused to answer that prayer immediately. He pleaded with God to allow him enter the land of Canaan but God refused. 1,500 years later, those prayers kept on surfacing before God. When Christ came, about 1,500 years later, God could no longer refuse Moses' words of prayers. So, in Matthew 17:1-3 God revealed that He answered Moses' prayers and allowed him to enter into the Promised Land.

"And after six days Jesus taketh Peter, James, and John his brother, and bringeth them up into an high mountain apart, and was transfigured before them: and his face did shine as the sun, and his raiment was white as the light. And, behold, there appeared unto them Moses and Elias talking with him" *(Matthew 17:1-3).*

No matter how long your words take before manifestation, do not give up even at the very point of death. Words of true believers are as decrees.

"And Elijah the Tishbite, who was of the inhabitants of Gilead, said unto Ahab, As the LORD God of Israel liveth, before whom I stand; there shall not be dew nor rain these years, but according to my word" *(1 Kings 17:1).*

Some decrees may put you into trouble but do not give up. It happened to Elijah, but he prevailed over all the forces of darkness that opposed his words. You only have to speak out and believe when you say things as the Lord commanded. It is a decree and it must stand.

In the days of Ezekiel, God took him to a valley of dry bones. When the hand of God comes upon you, it can take you to a place you do not like; a place where you are confronted by hopeless situations. God may choose to take you to a lifeless valley; to people, who have been abandoned in the valley of life. God can take you to people, who have lost all good things of their lives. It could be people, who may not be ready to respond to the gospel immediately. It could as well be people, who may be dead spiritually. When the hand of God is upon you, you have to prophesy to your destiny.

"So I prophesied as I was commanded: and as I prophesied, there was a noise, and behold a shaking, and the bones came together, bone to his bone" (Ezekiel 37:7).

Millions of people have died and were buried with unspoken decrees. When you refuse to say what you are supposed to say, some good things may actually die off in your life spiritually. The life and ministry of Jeremiah almost ended in a failure. He taught that he has finished all God called him. So, he concluded that there was no more need to pray. He even concluded there was no need to live any longer, judging from the situation that surrounded him.

"Moreover the word of the LORD came unto Jeremiah the second time, while he was yet shut up in the court of the prison, saying, Thus saith the LORD the maker thereof, the LORD that formed it, to establish it; the LORD is his name; Call unto me, and I will answer thee, and shew thee great and mighty things, which thou knowest not" (Jeremiah 33:1-3).

If you do not start decreeing now, you may actually die while it is not God's will. If you do not decree a thing now concerning your marriage, you may not marry or be married at all when you are supposed to marry. If you do not open your mouth and decree a thing now, evil people's decrees against your life would end up manifesting in your life. If you refuse to terminate the operations of the wicked over your life, obviously, they would continue. If cannot conclude that enough is enough, then evil works may never be eliminated in your life. You may be failing when you decided to remain a spectator. You need to begin to say things into existence. Do not allow yourself to be distracted.

A certain man got an opportunity to be with Christ under the same roof for many years. He ate in the same place with him, and traveled around with Christ for three good years. He was highly gifted in writing and never wrote useless things. He did not spend his time promoting newspapers that advertised nude pictures or wrote economics-made-easy. He never chased after great world leaders to write their speeches. He wrote so many things about God, the Holy Spirit and Christ.

In one of the gospels, John wrote and referred to Jesus as the son of God, son of man, divine actor, great soul winner, great physician, bread of life, water of life, defender of the weak, light of the world, the good shepherd, prince of life, King, servant, counselor, true vine, giver of the Holy Ghost, great intercessor, model sufferer, uplifted Savior, conqueror of death and restorer of the penitent.

He was the author of the gospel according to John, the first, second and the third epistles of John, and he finally authored the last book of the Bible, which is the book of Revelation. He identified himself with other believers during Domitian's great persecution, who was also a Roman emperor. John was arrested, detained and thrown into a boiling drum of oil. But he came out of the boiling oil alive. Finally, he was imprisoned at the isle of Patmos where he was expected to be eaten up by wild and sea animals. He was about 90 years old at that time and Christ appeared to him and gave him the accurate revelatory account of the end times.

Jesus commanded John to write down all he would see and hear, and he did. John's writing became the famous book of Revelation. But when John wrote up to the 17th chapter, something happened. The queen of heaven, the mother of all abominations upon the earth, distracted him. So, John abandoned his God's given assignment to admire this evil woman. What he needed to do was to decree against this evil woman, but his admiration for this mother of all harlots increased greatly instead. When he needed to decree a word, he could not. Sadly, John dropped his writing materials to admire an enemy of God, a woman that was sitting upon people's destinies, marriages, businesses, etc.

Before he could come back to himself and pick up his writing materials, it was almost late. Thank God that an angel of God intervened and spoke on his behalf. Your ministry, marriage, business or career could remain in mess if you continue to remain quiet, refusing to speak. Open your mouth and decree a thing. John's ministry would have been aborted had the angel of God not spoken on his behalf. We all may not get the chance for an angel of God to speak for us all the time. That is why it is so important that you learn how to decree for yourself.

"And I saw the woman drunken with the blood of the saints, and with the blood of the martyrs of Jesus: and when I saw her, I wondered with great admiration. And the angel said unto me, wherefore didst thou marvel? I will tell thee the mystery of the woman, and of the beast that carrieth her, which hath the seven heads and ten horns. And he saith unto me, the waters which thou sawest, where the whore sitteth, are peoples, and multitudes, and nations, and tongues" (Revelation 17:6-7, 15).

Many believers still approach prayers from a spectator's point of view rather than participatory. It is not profitable to attend prayer meetings to watch how people prayer instead of participating in praying. That is why great ministers and ministries have converted more attendees and admirers of prayer than participators. You must learn how to utter decrees without being apologetic. If John, who knew so much about Christ, could be affected in such a manner, and almost lost his ministry, then we must be careful. We must be watchful and re-examine our lives always.

Are you sure, you are still in the ministry that God put you? Have you been distracted by worldly cares and material things, without reference to Christ? Have you been building empires for yourself or for Christ? If John, who saw resurrected and glorified Christ, could come so close to loosing his ministry, then we must watch out for ourselves. Have you stopped praying and decreeing as you were commanded?

"Remove not the ancient landmark, which thy fathers have set"(Proverbs 22:28).

In the days of ancient prophets, they never closed their mouths or stopped believing God until miracles took place and their words confirmed. No one or any situation was able to distract them, not even dire consequences that trailed their lives. Nothing could change their convictions. They stopped the rain, and prayed down rain. The threats of Ahab or Jezebel, and their likes, did not shake. They did not give up easily. The dryness of the earth was not enough evidence to prove their prophecies were defeated. They believed God for change, regardless of how long afflictions continued.

"And Elijah said unto Ahab, Get thee up, eat and drink; for there is a sound of abundance of rain. So, Ahab went up to eat and to drink. And Elijah went up to the top of Carmel; and he cast himself down upon the earth, and put his face between his knees, And said to his servant, Go up now, look toward the sea. And he went up, and looked, and said, there is nothing. And he said, Go again seven times. And it came to pass at the seventh time, that he said, Behold, there ariseth a little cloud out of the sea, like a man's hand. And he said, Go up, say unto Ahab, Prepare thy chariot, and get thee down, that the rain stop thee not. And it came to pass in the mean while, that the heaven was black with clouds and wind, and there was a great rain. And Ahab rode, and went to Jezreel" (1 Kings 18:41-45).

Those who know how to decree a thing do not give up easily. They do not regard of evil reports, regardless of how evident they seem. They always win, in life or in death. Such people believe in asking, seeking and receiving, and do not subscribe to failures. Even after death, they are still winners.

"Ask, and it shall be given you; seek, and ye shall find; knock, and it shall be opened unto you: For every one that asketh receiveth; and he that seeketh findeth; and to him that knocketh it shall be opened" (Matthew 7:7-8).

At dying hours, people, who know how to decree according to God's Word, still trust God for miracles. They understand there is only one physical life, and are determined to live their physical lives to the glory of God. Such people do not believe in cheap means of success. Nothing can separate such people from the love they have for Christ. Even as they go through tribulations and persecutions, words of decree remain evident in their mouths. In distresses, they do not surrender to the wishes of their enemies. In famine and persecution, they decree words of faith. In nakedness and peril, they remain steadfast. Death, life, angels, principalities or powers can never persuade them change their love for Christ. Even in prosperity, people of decree continue with continuous decrees of faith, while maintain positive outlook about life.

CHAPTER SIX

People of Faith & Decrees

In the Bible days, many people were known for their faith and decrees. That is why they successfully obtained good reports while standing for God and His Word. Through faith, each of these people understood that world was framed by the Word of God. So, they knew that things, which were in existence, were made by Words spoken by God.

While spoken words give birth to things which cannot be seen with ordinary eyes, unspoken words remain largely unprofitable. People of faith and decrees speak words and believe in those words, regardless of any prevailing situation. Such people have absolute faith in God. God remains God for such people, in all situations. For instance, Abel believed in excellent sacrifice of love and thanksgiving to God, more than his brother, Cain did. That was why God accepted his sacrifice, that he even spoke at the point of his death. Death and its pains could not hinder Abel's cries to God. He kept speaking the same words, living the same life of righteousness until he left this world.

"Through faith we understand that the worlds were framed by the word of God, so that things which are seen were not made of things which do appear. By faith Abel offered unto God a more excellent sacrifice than Cain, by which he obtained witness that he was righteous, God testifying of his gifts: and by it he being dead yet speaketh" (Hebrews 11:3-4).

There was another man called Enoch. God took him to eternity without tasting death. Scriptures recorded that he was a man who lived a righteous life, which was absolutely focused on God alone. He lived a life of absolute obedience to God, which he decreed continually, until the day he was translated out of this world. It was by faith that he was able to decree and lived a kind of life that pleased God. Without faith, no one can decree a thing and hold on to it till the time appointed for it to happy. The twin brothers, Jacob and Esau, almost killed themselves while fighting in their mother's womb to receive a spoken word that will come to pass in their lives. Jacob was favored when the spoken word came.

Isaac's blessings were received through spoken words and decree. In order words, spoken words were the source of his prosperity. Isaac understood that things that existed during his lifetime were results of words his father either spoke or received from God. That was why it was unnecessary, for the people of that time, to struggle over Isaac's inheritance and blessings. The people of that time never struggled over resources or substances. They wanted words of decree in faith, not material things that would perish.

Material things perish, investments disappear but words of faith do not perish. You may not be able to carry your properties from place to place. You can also lose valuable investments and all that you have acquired in life. But spoken words of faith and decree are never lost. They live inside you. You do not need to pay anything to receive a spoken word. You can travel with it, sleep with it, live or die with it. Though not weighty physically, spoken words of faith and decree are weighty spiritually.

That was what Esau fought for, but Jacob got it. That is what we should fight for and that is what God wants us to get. Those who received words of faith and decree never failed, but those who lost it never succeeded. Therefore, people who failed in life and those who would yet fail would be because of not getting or loosing words of faith and decree.

Certificates and inheritances are good, but the efficacy of spoken words of faith is far-fetched. People succeed and fail, largely, because of words that were spoken concerning them. Nevertheless, more importantly is what people say about themselves. Are you living by what others said about you or by what God said concerning you? Have you ever said anything good to yourself or are you depending on what people said? What words are ruling your life? The words of men or the Word of God? Are you living by decrees of your ancestors or decrees of witches and wizards?

Esau lost his battle because he did not speak any word of decree into his life. Jacob took Esau's position and his name appeared among the people of faith because he decreed before he death.

> "By faith Jacob, when he was dying, blessed both the sons of Joseph; and worshipped, leaning upon the top of his staff" (Hebrews 11:21).

Beloved, before you die, pronounce a decree over your life. Decree over your children, like Jacob did, even at the point of death and believe it. Simply open your mouth and speak of faith, in agreement with the Word of God. That is what we mean by decree. Words of decrees of fervent Christians are not ordinary words. They are effective and they live forever more.

You are either condemned or justified by your words. You cannot afford to blame anyone for your failure. If you have ever received any negative words like Esau, you can revoke it. My advice is – take decrees seriously. Even Isaac told Esau so.

> *"And by thy sword shalt thou live, and shalt serve thy brother; and it shall come to pass when thou shalt have the dominion, that thou shalt break his yoke from off thy neck" (Genesis 27:40).*

The weapons of our warfare are not carnal. We succeed and fail by our words, and words we allow or disallow. You shall decree a thing and it shall be established. However, when you do not decree anything, it is possible that you will never be established. When other people's words concerning you, which are evil, are established in your life, you are doomed.

There was a time people looked at Joseph and said, this one is already dead. But even at that pitiful condition, Joseph was able to mention something by faith. He spoke by faith and decreed into his life and God honored it. The Bible recorded that before he died, he gave command concerning his bones.

"By faith Joseph, when he died, made mention of the departing of the children of Israel; and gave commandment concerning his bones" (Hebrews 11:22).

There are so many families where spirits of pharaoh and Egypt do exist. In such families, you need faith and words of decree to give birth to a person like Moses. There are places that male children cannot survive for three months, that is if they are allowed to be born at all. Parents, who found themselves in such cities, need faith and words of decrees to make it through. People, who give birth to divine children like Moses in the land of Egypt, must not be afraid of the words of the king. They must not listen to the devil's words or decrees of the king.

"Choosing rather to suffer affliction with the people of God, than to enjoy the pleasures of sin for a season" (Hebrews 11:25).

Those who possess words of decree do not stay permanently in wrong places. It is so easy for them to reject honors and promotions coming from evil people. They would choose to suffer instead of living in sin. They would prefer to take sides with God, rather than enjoying the pleasures of sin for a season. They would rather choose to suffer a reproach for Christ's sake than to enjoy the treasures of the Egyptians. They are ready to forsake their 'Egypt' (bondage), not minding how Pharaoh (bond master) would feel.

The beauty of living on words of faith and decree is that you could see, with your eyes of faith, invisible things that were spoken, which are yet to come. But nothing can be seen of unspoken words of decrees. When God spoke to Moses to take the route of Red Sea, he followed God's instruction until the children of Israel arrived at the shores of Red Sea. Moses was not afraid of the Red Sea because the God who created the Red Sea is his God.

By faith, the children of Israel passed through the Red Sea as in dry land. Their enemies, the Egyptians, who tried to do the same without faith, were all drowned. Again, when they approached the walls of Jericho, all hope was lost. But they remembered their God, who could do all things. In the presence of that wall of hindrance, they applied action to their faith. The children of Israel moved around the walls for seven good times, as God commanded them to do, and the walls fell flat.

> *"By faith the walls of Jericho fell down, after they were compassed about seven days"* *(Hebrews 11:30).*

It was like a dream but it was true. Their God is a God of miracles, signs and wonders. They knew that He had done it before and trusted that He would do it again. It was not hard for them to believe God. They walked round the mighty walls of Jericho and it fell down.

When they found themselves in Egypt, the Lord multiplied them. When a decree of death was passed against all Hebrew male children, the Lord spared Moses' life. When Pharaoh became angry with Moses that he ran away, the Lord called him in the wilderness and sent him back to Pharaoh. When they were leaving Egypt, God gave them favor in the sight of the Egyptians. When their water became bitter, the Lord changed it. When they became hungry in the wilderness, He gave them Manna from heaven. When the Amalek confronted them, the Lord gave them victory. When Moses died, God raised Joshua to take them to the Promised Land. If you remember God and trust Him, evil walls and words over your life shall fall flat. You shall decree a thing today and it shall be established to you.

When you believe God, no evil decree will affect you. That was what saved a harlot called Rahab. In the book of people of faith and decree, Gideon was remembered. He was a destroyer of evil altars, as well as builder of Holy altars. Gideon was a killer of the men of Succoth. There was also Daniel, a man filled with power for achievement. We also saw Barak and Samson.

Samson was a man, who had power over men and lions. Jephthah also was mentioned among the people of faith and decrees. After him was David, who was anointed instead of his brethren, and chosen in place of Saul. David was a man, who challenged Goliath and killed him. He won the love of Jonathan, the first son of his greatest enemy, Saul. David was a man, who survived various attempts to his life by his king.

By faith, David had victory over the Philistines, and was delivered from Saul's plans to trap him at Keilah. He listened to Abigail and had mercy on Nabal. At Ziph, God delivered again him from Saul. By faith, he obtained Ziklag from Achish and recovered all his lost from the Amalekites who invaded Ziklag and took all.

By faith, David went to Hebron by divine command and there, he was anointed king over the house of Judah. And finally, he was anointed king over all Israel at Hebron. He returned the ark of the Lord and humbled himself greatly before the Lord. David recovered the borders lost by his people and subdued the Philistines. David destroyed Ammon, received victory over Absalom, prepared his kingdom and died in peace at an old age.

In the history of people of faith and decrees, we saw Samuel whose birth was announced by an angel of God. An established Prophet from childhood and a man who escaped from Saul, Samuel prospered in Israel and died in the Lord at an old age. After him are all the prophets. Most of these people of faith and decrees subdued kingdoms, restored righteousness, obtained promises, stopped mouths of lions, quenched violence of fire, escaped edges of swords, were made strong in weaknesses, waxed strong in battles and chased armies of the aliens. Among these people of faith and decree are people of weaker vessels also.

"Women received their dead raised to life again: and others were tortured, not accepting deliverance; that they might obtain a better resurrection: And others had trial of cruel mocking and scourging, yea, moreover of bonds and imprisonment: They were stoned, they were sawn asunder, were tempted, were slain with the sword: they wandered about in sheepskins and goatskins; being destitute, afflicted, tormented; (Of whom the world was not worthy:) they wandered in deserts, and in mountains, and in dens and caves of the earth. And these all, having obtained a good report through faith, received not the promise" (Hebrews 11:35-39).

CHAPTER SEVEN

Deliverance Decrees

The only people that were empowered to pass decrees are God's true children. A believer's decree is the most effectual decree on earth. A decree of a one true believer can affect the entire people on earth, including all the seen and unseen forces. Believers' decrees can open or close any door; loose or bind, kill or give life. The Word of God is a gift from God to man, and serves as contact point and weapon to pass a decree. We have previously discussed the believer's decree. One thing every believe ought to realize is that the Lord has given every believer an authority to bind and loose. The power to cast out demons and say anything and it takes place is believers' inheritance and rights.

"And out of the ground the LORD God formed every beast of the field and every fowl of the air; and brought them unto Adam to see what he would call them: and whatsoever Adam called every living creature that was the name thereof. And Adam gave names to all cattle, and to the fowl of the air; and to every beast of the field; but for Adam there was not found an help-meet for him" (Genesis 2:19-20).

God gave man the power of dominion from creation. Men can say anything and God honors them, especially when true Christians or true believers, who absolutely believe in God, say them.

"Verily I say unto you, whatsoever ye shall bind on earth shall be bound in heaven: and whatsoever ye shall loose on earth shall be loosed in heaven. Again I say unto you, that if two of you shall agree on earth as touching anything that they shall ask, it

shall be done for them of my Father which is in heaven" (Matthew 18:18-19).

In the next chapter, we will be discussing 35 dangerous decrees that can help true believers recover and possess their possessions. It is worthy to note here that whosoever wishes to get involved in these decrees must first give himself or herself to God. It is a prerequisite that you are a born again believer before these prayers could work for you. You have to confess your sins and forsake them in order to prosper.

"He that covereth his sins shall not prosper: but whoso confesseth and forsaketh them shall have mercy" (Proverbs 28:13).

If you are still living in sin, then you cannot benefit from these decrees, for decrees also have potentials of backfiring on unrepentant sinners. After being sure of your salvation, and with resolve never go back to sin, you can then begin with praise and worship, and speaking in tongues, if possible. Start your prayers with thanksgiving to God for His goodness and mercy upon your life. Ask God to assist you by the power of His Holy Ghost. You can say these decrees as many times as the Spirit leads you. I recommend that you repeat these decrees as long as 6 or 12 months, as you are led. Select decrees that address your needs.

CHAPTER EIGHT

Deliverance Decrees (Part 1)

Business Decrees

In the prosperous name of our Lord Jesus Christ of Nazareth, Heavenly Father, I bless You for Your ultimate power to prosper. Therefore, I decree prosperity upon my life, upon my family and family members, upon my handwork. Henceforth, I nullify and terminate all satanic setbacks on my businesses. I decree that powers attacking my businesses shall die. Let the anger of God fall upon all satanic ventures in my business.

You my business, move forward as from today. I decree the removal of all satanic hindrances on my business. I decree death upon witchcraft attacks that were placed upon my business. I speak life upon my business. You my crippled business, arise, walk, jump and run fast. You my business, receive strength to prosper according to the Word of God.

"Beloved, I wish above all things that thou mayest prosper and be in health, even as thy soul prospereth" (3 John 1:2).

Therefore, prosper, prosper, and prosper by fire, in the name of Jesus. You, my business, whether the enemy likes it or not, prosper by fire and force. Move from failure to success, from darkness to light, from local to international. Now, my business, receive favor, even unmerited favors in the name of Jesus. Let me inform you, as from today, my business, begin to prevail, move from where you are now to where you are supposed to be all these years. My business shall not die and I decree that the eagle of my business shall fly henceforth, in the name of Jesus.

Let all the bewitchment against my business be frustrated forever. Any power that is limiting my businesses shall not succeed anymore. My business, hear me and hear me very well, you shall not die, and you shall not fold up. Debts shall not kill you. Your enemies shall fail. You will never be disgraced. No other business shall take your place. It is your time to prosper. I decree death upon evil powers that are polluting you.

O God, my businesses will no longer rob You of Your tithes and offerings. You, my business, begin to pay your tithes, give your offerings. Every curse upon my business shall die. O Lord, remove curses You have placed upon my businesses. By divine mercy and power, I take away every curse placed upon my businesses. Spirit of robbery and losses that follow my business around, die and die again. As from today, I will bring my tithes into the store house of God.

My businesses, receive open windows of heaven. I pour blessings into you. Every room in my business, begin to receive blessings. Let the power of God rebuke devourers for your sake. Any power that is devouring my business efforts, die immediately. My business shall excel beyond measure and limits. You, my business, I command you to reject geographical restrictions and expand beyond your boundaries.

Let your financial flow be steady. Do not give chances to failures again. Stand and fight for yourself. Bind and destroy all powers of darkness fighting against you. I decree that fires of prosperity shall fall upon you now. I decree freedom upon you from household wickedness. I command you to reject any grip of altars of darkness. Let the blood of Jesus redeem you now, in the name of Jesus Christ. Jesus of Nazareth, take over my business by fire. (After each decree, tell God what you want Him to do for you. Speak in tongues for as long as you remain in His presence).

Daily Decrees

By faith, all that Isaac said about Jacob and Esau concerning things to come took place. Therefore, I stand upon the Word of God, which says,

> *"Verily I say unto you, whatsoever ye shall bind on earth shall be bound in heaven: and whatsoever ye shall loose on earth shall be loosed in heaven"* *(Matthew 18:18).*

I bind any power that will attempt to spoil this day for me. You, my enemies of the day, I bind you with fetters of iron. I reject the spirit of tragedy today. You, my day, reject every progress diverter. I destroy the powers of the evil reporters and all satanic agents today. I recover this day from the grip of Satan. I decree that this day will mark the beginning of good days in my life. I decree death upon backwardness in this day. Divine whirlwind, I command you to fight against problems of this day. I decree death upon the evil planners. Let all distributors of shame carry away their shame today.

I decree that all my lost blessings shall be recovered today, in the name of Jesus.

O Lord, uphold my day and let all negative powers of this day receive self-destruction. You, my day, reject every form of disappointment, failures, manipulations and frustrations. Holy Ghost fire, possess my day. Blood of Jesus, flow into my day. Light of God, shine upon my day and destroy all territorial powers. Any power that is caging my day shall not survive today. I force my enemies to repent or receive the bread of affliction this day. I will make it this day, whether devil likes it or not.

This is the day of my promotion and no power can stop it henceforth. Lord Jesus, take over my day. I decree the absence of devil and all his agents in my life today. My life shall be guided completely this day. I refuse to meet with my enemies this day. If I must meet any of them, they shall bow to my God. My entire request this day shall be granted to the glory of God, in Jesus name I decree, Amen. (Start praying in tongues and spirit and begin to tell God what you want Him to do).

Environmental Decrees 1

I decree death upon any power in this environment that is against my visit. My mission in this place shall prosper and no power shall stand against me. I shall make it, whether enemies like it or not. I shall succeed in this place, in the name of Jesus. Evil powers that have sent others parking out of this place in shame shall not affect my life, for it is written,

"Blessed shalt thou be when thou comest in, and blessed shalt thou be when thou goest out"
(Deuteronomy 28:6).

As I come into this city, no power shall change the will of God for my life. I will live here and please my God all the days of my life. The Jezebels, Delilahs and agents of Satan in this environment shall not pull me down. I shall not be disgraced. Wasters of destines in this community, city and nation shall not waste my life. The blood of Jesus covers me. Fornicators and all the immoral boys and girls, including men and women will not write or appear in the last chapter of my life. As I come in, I shall be blessed, when I am going out, I shall be blessed. No power shall fool me in this place. Any power that will oppose me here shall die. I shall settle down and be established. The spirit of failure and destruction, or vagabond spirit shall not prevail over me. I shall prevail spiritually, physically, financially, materially, academically, socially, and mentally, in the name of Jesus.

I decree that all my mountains in this place shall be removed. I shall not spend my money in this place in vain. The demon in-charge of this place shall not rule over me. I shall rule over them and they shall bow to my God.

Blood of Jesus, speak destruction upon every negative power speaking against me in this place. I silence any power that refused to bow to Jesus Christ of Nazareth in this area. As you promoted Daniel in a strange land, O Lord, promote me here. Let the power that enabled Joseph to stand against sin in a strange land possess me now. I bind any power that will confront my righteousness and relationship with God in this area. I decree total victory over all my enemies in this place, day and night.

Because I am dwelling in the secret place of the most high, I shall abide under the shadow of the Almighty. In this area, I shall not fear the terrors by night or the arrows that fly by day. The pestilence that is walking in darkness and all the destruction wasting at noonday shall never see me. I hid myself under the blood of Jesus. No matter how enemies in this place are succeeding, they will not succeed over me. O Lord, be my habitation in this environment, I cover my dwelling place with the blood of Jesus.

Angels of the living God in this area, keep me in all my ways. Bear me up in your hands and do not allow me to dash my foot against a stone. I decree that all my prayers in this environment shall be answered. I will experience a closer relationship with God in this area. Difficult situations will become easy for me and impossibilities will become possible for me, in the mighty name of Jesus Christ of Nazareth.

O Lord, honor me in this place more than the indigenes and foreigners. Advertise Your glory in my life, family, and Ministry to Your own glory, in the mighty name of our Lord Jesus, Amen.

Decree Upon Children

As It is written,

"But thus saith the LORD, Even the captives of the mighty shall be taken away, and the prey of the terrible shall be delivered: for I will contend with him that contendeth with thee, and I will save thy children" (Isaiah 49:25).

I claim complete deliverance and full salvation for my children. O Lord, contend with evil powers that are contending with my children. All that Isaac said about Jacob and Esau came to pass. All that Jacob, by faith, also said concerning his children and grand children came to pass. By faith, all that I will say now concerning my children shall come to pass. By faith, I gather my children together; I begin to bless all my children.

I decree that none of my children shall continue in sin. I bind and cast out evil spirits of destruction and untimely deaths. My children will not suffer in the hands of Satan. I pull my children away from the hand of wicked spirits and satanic agents. O Lord, bless my children beyond my imagination. My children will never be manipulated by powers from the dark kingdom. Coffin spirits will not bury the destinies of my children.

Blood of Jesus, possess my children and deliver them from satanic markets and evil altars. Desert spirits, release all my children by fire and by force. By faith, I remove every satanic bullet in the lives of my children. O Lord, abort every evil in the lives of my children and deliver them from every evil. Every vagabond anointing upon my children, expire by fire.

I decree and declare that all my children will be great and mighty for Christ. Let divine tempest, seaquake, air quake and great earthquake deliver all my children from evil powers. I use brimstone and fire of God to deliver my children from every satanic captivity. I bind all evil powers that are assigned to waste the lives of my children. Hail and fire, mingled with the blood of the lamb, burn every problem that has refused to let my children go.

You, enemies of my children, receive great confusion. I deliver my children from the wicked powers of household wickedness. The stars of my children shall not wonder about. All the eagles of my children shall fly to the glory of God. As God stood with Daniel and promoted him, so shall all my children be supported and promoted by God. I decree that all my children shall represent God everywhere they go in their lives. Idols of any kind, place and time will not hold down my children. Poisons will be as vitamin for my children, when attempts is made to their lives. My children will live long in prosperity as commanded by God. No occult arrow shall enter into any of my children, it shall backfire. All my children shall make it, whether the enemy likes it or not, in the mighty name of Jesus.

Decree For Your Deliverance

In the anointed name of our Lord Jesus Christ of Nazareth, Father, I decree for my total deliverance. As it is written,

"But upon mount Zion shall be deliverance, and there shall be holiness; and the house of Jacob shall possess their possessions" (Obadiah 1:17).

I come unto mount Zion and I receive complete deliverance, holiness, and I possess my possession by fire. O Lord, who delivered Paul and Silas, deliver me this day. Any wicked power hindering my complete deliverance, I decree death unto your kingdom. My deliverance in the hands of powers of darkness, I release you by fire by force. I decree words of deliverance upon my life. Let my life embrace deliverance of God now. Blood of Jesus Christ of Nazareth, deliver me by fire. I decree that deliverance shall take place in every aspect of my life now. Every organ of my body, I lay my hands upon you now, receive perfect deliverance. Any power, holding me captive, receive destruction and release me. I take my deliverance by fire.

Let the anger of the Lord move into my life and destroy every evil structure erected against my life. I decree immediately that unbearable heat of the Almighty shall attack every evil power holding me in bondage. I command every disorderliness in my life to receive immediate order now. Every satanic poison inside my body, dry up by fire. I decree the death of arrows of fruitless efforts that has been fired into my life.

Powers of late progress, prospering in my life, receive double destruction immediately. Any power assigned to steal my deliverance, die immediately, in the mighty name of Jesus, Amen.

Decree For Your Destiny

It is written,

"For I am the LORD, I change not; therefore ye sons of Jacob are not consumed" (Malachi 3:6).

I am a child of God because I am born again. My destiny shall not be amputated. I decree that my divine destiny will appear and let perverted destiny disappear. I decree death upon satanic hands in my destiny. Let all powers of darkness assigned to monitor my destiny, receive blindness. I scatter every evil altar holding down my destiny and I break every curse of backwardness placed upon my destiny. My destiny, manifest by fire. I decree death upon all destiny killers and hijackers.

For it is written, "No weapon that is formed against thee shall prosper; and every tongue that shall rise against thee in judgment thou shalt condemn. This is the heritage of the servants of the LORD, and their righteousness is of me, saith the LORD" (Isaiah 54:17).

I destroy every weapon of destiny killers. I release rains of affliction upon all destiny destroyers that are after my life. Let the eyes of evil observers be blinded by fire. Let all poverty activators that are attacking my life be disgraced, in the name of Jesus. Let all forest demons released against my destiny return in shame. Every iron-like curse, placed upon my life to render my destiny useless, break into pieces now. Every evil embargo placed upon my destiny, be lifted now. I decree death upon all enemies of my destiny. I command all dark agents and wicked broadcasters attacking my destiny to attack themselves. O Lord, deliver every aspect of my destiny today and forever, in the name of Jesus.

Decree During Child-Bearing

You my body, you are productive and fertile for child bearing. By the power of God, you are fruitful, no matter what devil is doing. I decree to the power of darkness that I am not barren.

For it is written,

"And God blessed them, and God said unto them, be fruitful, and multiply, and replenish the earth, and subdue it: and have dominion over the fish of the sea, and over the fowl of the air, and over every living thing that moveth upon the earth" (Genesis 1:28).

My family will be fruitful and blessed and divinely favored. The scriptures cannot be broken, so I will multiply and replenish the earth. No power from the water or air shall overcome me. I have dominion over the entire creatures. Every water spirit is subject to me. The power of God upon my life is above every other power. Greater is He that is in me than he that is in the whole world. The works of all occult people in the world are useless because I am a child of God.

Therefore, I decree there will be no abortion. I reject every sexual demon. I break covenant with spirit marriages, and I put to an end every eating in my dreams and every remote-control mechanisms. Let every intercourse with demonic sexual partners be terminated immediately. Every agent of miscarriage and attacks during pregnancies, die. I decree complete destruction of fibroids, ovarian cysts, satanic growths, cancer and every evil plantation in my life. I remove all impediments in my birth canal by fire. Every peppery arrow, enchantments, marital disgrace, satanic poisons, etc., living inside my body, be washed by the blood of Jesus. I purge you out by fire, in the mighty name of Jesus. Amen.

Decree Against Academic Defeats

It is written,

"It pleased Darius to set over the kingdom an hundred and twenty princes, which should be over the whole kingdom; And over these three presidents; of whom Daniel was first: that the princes might give accounts unto them, and the king should have no damage. Then this Daniel was preferred above the presidents and princes, because an excellent spirit was in him; and the king thought to set him over the whole realm" (Daniel 6:1-3).

The God that placed Daniel in first position is my God. I decree that I shall be preferred above all the people around me. I shall win in every competition. Because I am born again, I have an excellent spirit. I am serving God of excellence. In every exam, I will satisfy my examiners beyond their requirements. I will give correct answers to every question. Failure is not my portion and I will make it academically. As for me, I decree that all my competitors will go behind me and I refuse to go behind or go backwards in life.

For it is written, "And the LORD shall make thee the head, and not the tail; and thou shalt be above only, and thou shalt not be beneath; if that thou hearken unto the commandments of the LORD thy God, which I command thee this day, to observe and to do them" (Deuteronomy 28:13).

I am on the top and I will remain on top forever, for it is where the Lord placed me. No power can bring me down and as for me, I cannot be the tail. I will be above only, and not beneath. Anything that will try to bring me down academically shall die. You my brain, reject memory failures. I receive distinctions because the Lord has destined me for the best. I am singled out to make it academically.

Blood of Jesus, flow into my academic foundation. Holy Ghost Fire, burn inside my brain and clean every impurity. I decree death upon any power stealing information from me during exams. Spirit of death and hell, release my academic breakthroughs by fire, in the mighty name of Jesus.

Decree For Employment

"But my God shall supply all your need according to his riches in glory by Christ Jesus" (Philippians 4:19).

I stand upon the Word of God and decree for immediate release of my employment now. O Lord, give me a job that will give me the opportunity to serve You more. Let all my needs and others be supplied through the new job, in the name of Jesus. I receive the power to be rich for the Lord. By the power in the name of Jesus Christ, I come against all demons against my employment and are hindering me from being employed in the right place.

You, wicked demons, I bring the blood of Jesus against your power. I release my employment from your grip, in Jesus name. From now on, I reject the spirit of unemployment. I receive my employment letter by force, in the mighty name of Jesus Christ. I bind every spirit of unemployment and I loose my job from their hands. I claim my employment now. I chain all powers against my employment together and I cast all you powers into eternal darkness. I imprison you now with the judgment key never to escape again until the judgment day of the Lord, in the name of Jesus. I cover and protect my job with the blood of Jesus.

For it is written,

"And they overcame him by the blood of the Lamb and by the word of their testimony; and they loved not their lives unto the death" (Revelation 12:11).

Every spirit of unemployment, I overcome you now by the blood of the Lamb and by the word of my testimony. I command you to bow forever in my life, in the mighty name of Jesus Christ of Nazareth, Amen.

CHAPTER NINE

Deliverance Decrees (Part 2)

Decree Against Marital Failures

I decree that my marriage will not fail, whether devil likes it or not. I stand against evil powers fighting against my marriage. I command them to fail woefully now by the power of God. Let every evil spirit fostering marital breakup in my foundation be frustrated, in the mighty name of Jesus. By the power in the blood of Jesus, I nullify every evil mark placed upon my marriage, in the mighty name of Jesus. I frustrate the powers that have been assigned to destroy my marriage and I command them to die by fire now.

O Lord, God of Abraham, Isaac and Jacob, deliver my marriage from destruction and give me marital success by fire, in the name of Jesus. Blood of Jesus, flow into my marriage and cleanse every evil deposit in my marital home, in the name of Jesus.

For it is written,

"See, I have this day set thee over the nations and over the kingdoms, to root out, and to pull down, and to destroy, and to throw down, to build, and to plant" (Jeremiah 1:10).

Let all local or international spirits of marital failures that are attacking my marriage be rooted out by the power in the Word of God. Let your foundation be destroyed, in the mighty name of Jesus Christ of Nazareth. I throw down evil altars of marital failures in my life, in the mighty name of Jesus. I build and plant my marriage in the solid rock of ages, the Lord Jesus Christ. O Lord, uphold my marriage by Your power, in the mighty name of Jesus.

Decree For Your Prayer Life

I decree fire on my prayer life. Let the anointing of fire and prayerfulness fall upon my prayer altar, in the name of Jesus. O Lord, help me to receive the power to pray without ceasing. Any power attacking my prayer life, wherever you are, I say to you, die, die, die, in the mighty name of Jesus. Blood of Jesus, fall upon my tongue and Let the anointing for prayer arrest my spirit, soul and body now, in the mighty name of Jesus. Power to pray and fast, possess me by fire. From today, I convert my weakness to strength, spiritually and physically. You my life, whether you feel like praying or not, begin to pray. I receive the power to speak in tongues now.

For it is written,

"And he that searcheth the hearts knoweth what is the mind of the Spirit, because he maketh intercession for the saints according to the will of God" (Romans 8:27).

Spirit of the living God, help my infirmities now, in the name of Jesus. Spirit of Christ, I beg you to help me to be prayerful. Blessed Holy Spirit, begin to intercede for me by Your mercies. Every spiritual weakness that is attacking my prayer life, die by fire, in the name of Jesus. Let my tongue be converted into fire and let my prayers be by the leading of the Holy Spirit. I decree complete death to all evil powers attacking my prayer life from the waters. Blood of Jesus, speak destruction to prayerlessness spirit operating in my life, in the mighty name of Jesus. Amen.

Decree To Protect Your Profession

Any evil decree that was passed to destroy my profession, I revoke you, in the mighty name of Jesus. Every evil gang-up against my profession, scatter by fire, in the name of Jesus. O Lord, save my profession from powers of destruction. Every enemy of my profession, be exposed and be disgraced, in the name of Jesus. Any power from my place of birth and from my parents, assigned to divert me to a wrong profession, kill yourselves now, in the mighty name of Jesus. Any power that is fighting to make me useless in this life, fail woefully without mercy now.

As God declared my goodness, so shall it be whether the enemy likes it or not. Holy Ghost fire, burn all the evil powers fighting against my profession to ashes, in the mighty name of Jesus.

For it is written,

"Then this Daniel was preferred above the presidents and princes, because an excellent spirit was in him; and the king thought to set him over the whole realm" (Daniel 6:3).

I decree that I will be preferred above all my equals in my profession, in the mighty name of Jesus. I receive the power of excellence to prevail over all my contemporaries forever and ever, in the mighty name of Jesus. Spirit of perfection, posses me all through my life by fire. I refuse to give up. My enemies shall give up. Blood of Jesus, Holy Ghost fire, deliver my profession from household enemies. Let evil altars erected against my profession, local or international, collapse by fire now, in the name of Jesus.

Decree Against Stubborn Situations

By the power in the name of Jesus, I decree death upon all stubborn situations in my life, in the mighty name of Jesus. You, stubborn situation, you cannot resist God, I command you to die by the power of God now. Let every pillar of stubborn situation in my life be dismantled now, in the name of Jesus. You, Pharaoh in my life, enter into the Red Sea and die. Every satanic embargo that is placed upon my life, be lifted by force now, in the mighty name of Jesus.

For it is written in the book of Jeremiah, "See, I have this day set thee over the nations and over the kingdoms, to root out, and to pull down, and to destroy, and to throw down, to build, and to plant" (Jeremiah 1:10).

I stand against nations and kingdoms of evil situations in my life. I break every yoke of stubborn situation in my life by the power of God. I root out every root of evil situation in my life. Let all evil powers that are backing up problems in my life begin to destroy themselves now. Holy Ghost fire, fight for me. Blood of Jesus, fight for me. In the name of Jesus, I remove the strength of stubborn situations in my life now. God of deliverance, deliver me from the powers of stubborn situations, in the mighty name of Jesus.

For it is written,

"Behold, I give unto you power to tread on serpents and scorpions, and over all the power of the enemy: and nothing shall by any means hurt you" *(Luke 10:19).*

Therefore, I receive power to tread on all stubborn situations in my life from today and forever and ever, in the name of Jesus.

Decree For Open-Heaven

Let destroying flood of the Almighty destroy every power blocking my heavens. I decree immediate opening of my heavens now, in the name of Jesus. O Lord, let raging fire from You burn all evil instruments blocking my heavens to ashes. By the decree of the Almighty, I open my heavens with divine whirlwind. I decree immediate destruction to the queen of heaven, who is blocking my heavens. Divine air quakes and godly tempest, open up my heavens by fire.

For it is written,

"Oh that thou wouldest rend the heavens, that thou wouldest come down, that the mountains might flow down at thy presence" (Isaiah 64:1).

Father Lord, rend the heavens for my sake and come down that the mountains might flow down at Your presence. Holy Ghost fire, burn all satanic roadblocks that are mounted on my way to my heavens. I claim the miracles to open-heaven. Let my life begin to experience the joy of open-heaven from today, in the mighty name of Jesus Christ of Nazareth.

Blood of Jesus flow into my life and let my heaven and earth open by fire now. You my life, begin to operate in an open-heaven environment. I release thunder and fire, red-hot charcoal and anger of God against marine powers that are blocking my heavens. Let confusion and divine disorderliness, frustrate the devil in my heavenlies. I bring disappointment and failures to all occult personalities using the heavenlies against me, in the name of Jesus.

Decree For Supernatural Breakthrough

Covenant keeping God, arise and fight for me, in the name of Jesus Christ. For it is written, "The earth is the LORD's, and the fullness thereof; the world, and they that dwell therein" (Psalms 24:1).

Therefore, I receive supernatural breakthrough, in the name of Jesus. By the power that formed the whole universe, I stand against powers that are attacking my divine connections and appointments. O Lord, give me immeasurable blessing from the third heavens. I receive the fullness of God's power to prosper. I break evil warehouses that are holding back my blessings with great earthquake. I send shock and death to water spirits that are holding back my supernatural breakthrough. I decree that my breakthrough shall no longer be delayed, in the mighty name of Jesus.

For it is written,

"Beloved, I wish above all things that thou mayest prosper and be in health, even as thy soul prospereth" (3 John 1:2).

Therefore, I decree that I shall prosper in and out henceforth, in Jesus name. With the destroying flood of God, I destroy enemies that are countering my supernatural breakthrough, in the name of Jesus. O Lord, promote me beyond my imagination. I command divine madness and death against the spirit of poverty in my life. Every altar of poverty in my life, be destroyed on all sides, in the mighty name of Jesus. I stand against manipulators of my breakthrough until they are no more. I command every evil traffic warden that is up against my breakthrough to fall down and die, in the name of Jesus, Amen.

Decree For Your Marriage

I decree death to all local and international powers of darkness fighting against my marriage. Any marriage that has been conducted on my behalf in the spirit realm, I reject you by fire. Let all evil and spiritual relationships in my life be terminated by fire, in the name of Jesus. Let all the spirit children, concubines and evil witnesses that are on assignment against my life, destroy themselves, in the name of Jesus.

For it is written,

"Nevertheless, to avoid fornication, let every man have his own wife, and let every woman have her own husband" (1 Corinthians 7:2).

O Lord, show me my life partner and lead me into a profitable marriage. Any sprit of immorality that has been assigned to waste my life, I waste you today. I decree death to overtake spirit of immorality in my life. Let all evil relationships that has been assigned to lead me into death be broken without consideration. I command every demon that prevents marriages to die immediately in my case, in the name of Jesus. Any evil and sinful partner that do not want to allow me to go, die, in the name of Jesus.

I wash my body, soul and spirit with the blood of Jesus. I decree that my glory, beauty, handsomeness shall appeal to my life partner. I decree that before the end of this program, my marriage shall appear by force. Lord Jesus, take me to my marital home and establish my marriage, in the name of Jesus.

Decree For Finance

I decree death over the spirit of poverty and spirit of financial quagmire and predicament. Let every blockade to my cash flow be lifted by force now immediately, in the name of Jesus. I release financial prosperity into my life and I decree that financially, I shall prosper forever.

For it is written,

"And the peace of God, which passeth all understanding, shall keep your hearts and minds through Christ Jesus. But my God shall supply all your need according to his riches in glory by Christ Jesus" (Philippians 4:7, 19).

O Lord, open an account for me in heaven and earth, and begin to supply all my needs according to Your riches in glory by Christ Jesus. Any demonic idol that is holding my money, release them now and be destroyed, in the name of Jesus. Let all demons arresting my finances be destroyed and my finances released now. Let all evil transfers of my blessings and finances be overturned now, as I recovered every transferred blessings and finances, in the name of Jesus Christ.

I decree immediate collapse of all satanic banks and destruction of all banks collecting my money illegally. I recover all my lost finances and I tear every rag of poverty in my life to pieces. Every household arrow of financial problems, backfire now. O Lord, use divine whirlwind to bring back all finances handed over to Satan by my ancestors. Let the unbearable heat of God burn every spiritual evil robber to death, in the mighty name of Jesus.

Decree For Sound Health

I decree that my health shall not fail, in the mighty name of Jesus. By the blood of Jesus, I recover my health from the altar of health destroyers, in the mighty name of Jesus. Fire of God, burn every disease and germs in my blood to ashes. Blood of Jesus, flow into my life and replace my blood with Yours. I take authority against every poison of sickness in my body, in the mighty name of Jesus.

For it is written, "If I shut up heaven that there be no rain, or if I command the locusts to devour the land, or if I send pestilence among my people; If my people, which are called by my name, shall humble themselves, and pray, and seek my face, and turn from their wicked ways; then will I hear from heaven, and will forgive their sin, and will heal their land" (2 Chronicles 7:13-14).

Let the heavens over my health be opened and I command good health to possess my life by fire. O Lord, release the rain of health upon my life. Let every demonic locust that is eating up my health die by force. Let all pestilence and sicknesses in my life be consumed by fire. I call upon the name of Jesus Christ to destroy sicknesses and infirmities in my blood. Let every root of sin in my life that has been given the power to promote sicknesses in my life dry up immediately by fire. Holy Ghost fire and blood of Jesus, come into my life and destroy the powers of sicknesses in my life.

Let destroying flood of God destroy all sicknesses in my body and soul. Let weaknesses that I have receive double destruction now. I release the anger of God upon the foundation of every sickness in my body. Let any sickness in my body eat the bread of affliction and die.

For it is written, "And they overcame him by the blood of the Lamb and by the word of their testimony; and they loved not their lives unto the death" (Revelation 12:11).

I overcome every illness with the blood of the lamb and by the word of my testimony and faith in Christ, in the name of Jesus.

Decree For Prosperity

Every agent of death in my life, die immediately by fire. Let the anointing that breaks every yoke in my life begin to terminate the ministry of lack in my life. Anger of God, descend on every wicked spirit challenging my prosperity and my life.

For it is written,

"The LORD shall open unto thee his good treasure, the heaven to give the rain unto thy land in his season, and to bless all the work of thine hand: and thou shalt lend unto many nations, and thou shalt not borrow" (Deuteronomy 28:12).

I stand on the Word of God and command that good treasures of God shall be opened for me. I decree that my heavens shall open to give rain into my land. Let doors of my prosperity begin to open by force, in the name of Jesus.

O Lord, bless the works of my hands. Every spirit of debts that has been assigned to destroy my life, die first.

For it is written,

"And the LORD shall make thee plenteous in goods, in the fruit of thy body, and in the fruit of thy cattle, and in the fruit of thy ground, in the land which the LORD swore unto thy fathers to give thee" (Deuteronomy 28:11).

Therefore, I receive the anointing of plenty of goods, plenty of fruits of my body, plenty of fruits of my cattle, plenty of fruits of the ground, and plenty in all areas of my life, in the name of Jesus. My basket and stores shall be filled to the glory of God. I shall not be cursed in the city. My going out and coming in shall be in prosperity.

Let over-flowing flood of the Almighty carry away lack and poverty, in the name of Jesus. I reject every counterfeit money that would launch poverty in my life. I reject and remove such money forever and ever. I command wind of deliverance to bring prosperity into my life and blow away poverty from my life as it is written,

"Beloved, I wish above all things that thou mayest prosper and be in health, even as thy soul prospereth" (3 John 1:2).

Decree For Long Life

I decree that I will live long in this world to please my God. Any power that says that I will not live long to the glory of God shall perish. I will not die but live to please God, in the mighty name of Jesus. Blood of Jesus, renew my life, and make me younger every day. I fire back every arrow of untimely death, in the name of Jesus.

For it is written,

"With long life will I satisfy him, and shew him my salvation" (Psalms 91:16).

Therefore, O Lord, satisfy me with long life and show me Your salvation in every area of my life, in the name of Jesus. Any power that is killing me little by little, wherever you are, begin to die now, in the mighty name of Jesus. Let that evil power that is feeding on my joy begin to feed with death and die forever and ever by fire. Blood of Jesus, flow into my foundation. Holy Ghost fire, burn into my foundation.

Let every property of death in my foundation be consumed by fire. Powers that kill young people and young things around me, receive bitter destruction, madness and death now, in the name of Jesus. I reject every curse of untimely death placed upon my life.

Every household arrow of premature death, backfire and kill your original owner. Let all evil properties of death that is prospering in my family expire by force. Powers that change the body, you are defeated in my life, therefore, die, die, die and die again. Let the blood of Jesus neutralize any poison of death inside my blood. O Lord, inject me with a quality of life that cannot be uttered forever and ever, in Jesus name. Amen.

Decree For Procreation

I was born as a baby, therefore I will give birth as well. A woman conceived me, and I am a seed of procreation. Therefore, I command the seed of procreation inside my body to begin to function by force. Any power that is making my body barren shall not succeed henceforth. You my body, become productive by force. I spread divine fertilizers on my body and I cause my body to respond and reproduce to the glory of God.

Now, you, spirit of death living inside my body, come out now and die by fire. Let all evil plantations in my body die, whatever God has planted in my life must grow to maturity and whatever devil has planted in my body must die immediately. Blood of Jesus, flow into my foundation and let my body and life begin to procreate now.

For it is written,

"And God blessed them, and God said unto them,
be fruitful, and multiply, and replenish the earth,
and subdue it: and have dominion over the fish of
the sea, and over the fowl of the air, and over every
living thing that moveth upon the earth" (Genesis
1:28).

Therefore, I claim all blessings of God for my life from the beginning. My marriage, business, spiritual and physical lives, etc., shall be fruitful as God has commanded. I will surely multiply, and good things will happen to my life this year, in the name of Jesus. I reject barrenness, wastage, impotency, miscarriage, abortion and all manner of demonic delays and destruction.

You, my life, begin to replenish and subdue the earth. I must have dominion over the powers of the sea, air, and over every living and non-living things to the glory of God. I loose my life from any demonic bondage, in the mighty name of Jesus.

Ministerial Decrees

I decree death to evil powers that are working against the calling of God in my life. Let death visit the pit of hell for my sake and recover my calling. Today, I decree that my ministry shall move forward by fire. Let the blood of Jesus remove every satanic limitation in my calling. As I open my mouth to minister, O Lord, confirm Your Word in my mouth.

For it is written,

"Thou shalt also decree a thing, and it shall be established unto thee: and the light shall shine upon thy ways" (Job 22:28).

Therefore, I decree life into my ministry immediately. As I stand to preach, people will repent in mass and wonderful testimonies will be recorded, in the name of Jesus.

For it is written,

"And Jesus answered and said unto him, Blessed art thou, Simon Barjona: for flesh and blood hath not revealed it unto thee, but my Father which is in heaven. And I say also unto thee, that thou art Peter, and upon this rock I will build my church; and the gates of hell shall not prevail against it. And I will give unto thee the keys of the kingdom of heaven: and whatsoever thou shalt bind on earth shall be bound in heaven: and whatsoever thou shalt loose on earth shall be loosed in heaven. Then charged he his disciples that they should tell no man that he was Jesus the Christ" (Matthew 16:17-20).

Therefore, I decree that as I minster, anywhere or at any time, there will be signs and wonders. Let there be salvation, conviction, confession, forsaking of sins, hatred for sin, decisions for Christ, sanctification, restitution and Holy Ghost baptism. As I minster, all manner of sicknesses and diseases shall disappear. People who are stricken by these ailments shall be delivered. Leprosy will go, the paralyzed will be let loose, and they will be set free.

Blindness, laziness, dumbness and lameness will all disappear, in the name of Jesus.

I decree that my ministration will destroy sin, cast out unclean spirits, plagues, issues of blood, will calm storms of life and bring peace to troubled souls. My ministration will raise the dead, destroy barrenness, feed hungry souls, turn water into wine, deliver the impotent and make people rich, in the name of Jesus, Amen.

Decree For Your Family Success

I decree that whether devil and his agents like it or not, my family shall succeed, in the name of Jesus. Other people may be failing in my family line but my own family shall not fail. I single my family out for great success, in the mighty name of Jesus. O Lord, prosper my family by Your power.

For it is written,

"And they overcame him by the blood of the Lamb, and by the word of their testimony; and they loved not their lives unto the death" (Revelation 12:11).

Therefore, I will overcome all demons attacking my family to the glory of God. Others may fail but I refuse to fail. I shall overcome by fire and by force. I reject parental curses and evil influence surrounding me henceforth. I reject every evil inheritance and I surrender my family to the family line of Jesus.

Separate my family from every evil pattern by fire and by force, O Lord. Divine whirlwind, take away my family from destruction. Fire of God, be ignited in my family and let thunder and fire protect my immediate family and distant families. Blood of Jesus, save my family from destruction and from wicked oppressors assigned to destroy us.

Divine and perfect unity, link my family members up again and again. I send arrows of destruction into the camp of my enemies in the land of the living and dead. You, stubborn enemies of my family, kill yourselves now. You, eagle of my family, begin to fly by fire, in the name of Jesus, Amen.

CHAPTER TEN

Deliverance Decrees (Part 3)

Decree For Promotion

By the power in the Blood of Jesus, I decree for my promotion by force. I stand against evil powers that are standing against my promotion to excellence. Let the anointing of divine promotion posses me now from local and international fronts, in the mighty name of Jesus.

For it is written,

"For promotion cometh neither from the east, nor from the west, nor from the south. But God is the judge: he putteth down one, and setteth up another" (Psalms 75:6-7).

Therefore, I claim divine promotion that comes directly from God. O Lord, promote me without delay. I decree that evil decisions against me shall backfire. Those who would fall for me to rise will not resist their fall. Therefore, I decree that they shall fall immediately, in the name of Jesus. Blood of Jesus, speak to my favor and promotion. Let my promotion be approved by blessed Holy Trinity, in the name of Jesus.

For it is written,

"Then the king promoted Shadrach, Meshach, and Abed-nego, in the province of Babylon" (Daniel 3:30).

Any king from any kingdom that has been assigned to promote me must promote me, whether he likes it or not. In a foreign land, I shall be promoted above my equals. Heavenly father, Lord Jesus, Blessed Holy spirit, promote me to Your glory. Every demon that is fighting my promotion, receive death and die.

I decree my promotion today and move from promotion to promotion. I refuse to stay long than required in any promotion, in the name of Jesus, Amen.

Environmental Decree 2

I decree death to all coastal powers in this land. Let evil powers in this land and environment be frustrated. Any power claiming the ownership of this land, be incapacitated by fire, in the name of Jesus.

For it is written,

"The earth is the LORD's, and the fullness thereof; the world, and they that dwell therein" (Psalms 24:1).

Therefore, I decree death to evil powers operating in this environment, which has refused to submit to the will of God. You, that power that wishes to dominate my environment, to destroy and control people and their activities against the will of God, die, in the mighty name of Jesus. I lift every evil embargo placed on my job and business in this land. I take away my prosperity and file from altars of darkness in this environment. Any power that wishes me evil in this place shall fail woefully.

Whatever I do in this land shall prosper, whether enemies like it or not. Power of God, arise and fight for me in this land. Blood of Jesus, speak for me in this place. I receive my freedom and breakthrough in this place, in the name of Jesus. I shall be established in this place against the will of Satan. The power that converts people to stand against God in this land shall not succeed in my life.

I receive power over the spirit of immorality and other popular and unpopular sins in this land. I refuse to be defiled or defeated in this land.

For it is written,

"Blessed shalt thou be when thou comest in, and blessed shalt thou be when thou goest out" *(Deuteronomy 28:6).*

Therefore, as I arrive in this land, I shall be blessed. As I go out when it is the perfect will of God, I shall be blessed. I refuse to overstay or under-stay in this land, in the name of Jesus, Amen.

Weekly Decree

This is my week, I will rule and reign over the powers of darkness in the name of Jesus. I decree paralysis and extreme destruction to any evil force that will arise against me this week. Let the door of prosperity open for me this week in the name of Jesus. By the anointing of God, I break every evil yoke over my life this week. I receive divine and unmerited favors this week. As I enter into this week, I recover all my lost items.

For it is written,

"Thou shalt also decree a thing, and it shall be established unto thee: and the light shall shine upon thy ways" (Job 22:28).

Therefore, I decree that the spirit of Pharaoh that is sitting on my destiny shall die this week. I shall enter into my promise land and all enemies and giants in the land shall die for my sake. I send confusion, double destruction and great furnace to all my enemies this week. This is my week of jubilee and my deliverance will not delay. As my enemies open their mouths against me this week, I command them to be shut. I command brimstone and fire to visit enemies of my progress, in the mighty name of Jesus. Wherever enemies gather today and throughout the week, I command fire of God, air-quake and great earthquake to visit them, in the name of Jesus.

My destiny shall move forward and my eagle shall fly as my stars arise with great brightness, in the name of Jesus. I decree that throughout this week, miracles, signs and wonders will overtake me, and my greatness will become visible by fire, in the name of Jesus, Amen.

Monthly Decree

By the decree of the Almighty, I claim my divine portion for this month. Let evil plans of enemies against me this month backfire. You, this month, before you go finally, release all my miracles, signs and wonders, in the mighty name of Jesus.

For it is written,

"Thou shalt also decree a thing, and it shall be established unto thee: and the light shall shine upon thy ways" (Job 22:28).

Therefore, I decree that this month shall be the month of my establishment, settlement, and prosperity. By the power that established Joseph in Egypt, I decree my establishment this month. Whether my Pharaoh likes it or not, it is written,

"That he would grant unto us, that we being delivered out of the hand of our enemies might serve him without fear, To give light to them that sit in darkness and in the shadow of death, to guide our feet into the way of peace" (Luke 1:74, 79).

Therefore, I am completely delivered from the hands of my enemies. I will serve my God better this month without fear. Light of Christ will shine in my darkness this month. Death will fail woefully in my life this month. All evil observers of my life this month shall be blinded. My progress shall not be diverted this month. The powers that arrest progresses will sleep permanently for my sake this month. My progress must appear, in the mighty name of Jesus.

I decree that my angel of this month will not delay my supplies. I decree death to demons contending with my angels of blessing. Death will be far from my family this month and evil will disappear from every member of my family this month. You, territorial spirits, be frustrated in this month. I bury all problems that would come my way in this month.

For it is written,

"Behold, I give unto you power to tread on serpents and scorpions, and over all the power of the enemy: and nothing shall by any means hurt you" (Luke 10:19).

Therefore, I receive power to destroy the powers of my enemies this month, in the name of Jesus, Amen.

Decree Upon The Season

Father Lord, thank You for Your great power over every season. I stand upon Your power and claim my blessings in this season. You, wicked powers that attack people in seasons, I am not your candidate. By the anointing of the Holy Ghost, I break the backbone of evil seasons. I decree death to all sicknesses and failures that normally attack me in seasons. O Lord, deliver me from demons attached to this season by fire, in the name of Jesus.

For it is written,

"To everything there is a season, and a time to every purpose under the heaven: A time to be born, and a time to die; a time to plant, and a time to pluck up that which is planted; A time to kill, and a time to heal; a time to break down, and a time to build up; A time to weep, and a time to laugh; a time to mourn, and a time to dance; A time to cast away stones, and a time to gather stones together; a time to embrace, and a time to refrain from embracing;

A time to get, and a time to lose; a time to keep, and a time to cast away; A time to rend, and a time to sew; a time to keep silence, and a time to speak; A time to love, and a time to hate; a time of war, and a time of peace" (Ecclesiastes 3:1-8).

Therefore, I claim all the good things that are meant for me in the season. I will receive my blessings exactly at right times in this season. All that God has purposed for me during this season shall manifest by fire. All good purposes of God for my life in this season shall not be diverted, in the mighty name of Jesus. I decree that all I needed to give birth during this season shall manifest by fire. Let all problems in my life die this season by the power in the blood of Jesus. I begin to plant prosperity into my life in this season. I decree that as I plant, I shall harvest all the good things I have planted before the end of this season. O Lord, this season will be favorable to me by fire, in the name of Jesus, Amen.

Decree Upon The Year

By the anointing of the Holy Ghost, I decree complete victory over all forces of my enemies in this year. Let the anger of God destroy the enemies of my progress this year. This is the year my prosperity shall manifest. Every pregnancy for good things in my life this year shall not be aborted, in the name of Jesus.

For it is written,

"Thou shalt also decree a thing, and it shall be established unto thee: and the light shall shine upon thy ways" (Job 22:28).

Therefore, I decree death to problems in my life this year. This is the year that all my enemies shall be put to death whether they like it or not. All that need to die this year for me to receive my deliverance to the glory of God must die. I shall be healed perfectly this year. I shall not break down emotionally, spiritually or physically in this year. Let all that need to fall for me to be able to rise up this year fall immediately. This is the year that I shall build up all that has been pulled down by devil in my life.

All that my ancestors have destroyed through idolatry shall be rebuilt this year. I decree death to anything that would cause me to weep and be sorrowful in my life this year. I shall laugh throughout the year to the glory of the Lord. Mourning will not come near me this year. This is the year I shall dance to the glory of God and to the shame of devil. Every evil shall be cast down and all my blessings shall be gathered together, in the name of the Almighty Jesus. (Decree this for 21 days in any month of your choice).

Decree Upon Your Investments

By the decree of God, I say yes to my investments. This time, I decree death to every demon fighting against my investments in this year. O Lord, begin to invest spiritual things in my life. Let all physical investments that are due in my life begin to take place, whether enemies like it or not. By the power in the blood of Jesus, I begin to invest in my business, marriage, family, and academics and in all areas of my life.

For it is written,

"The LORD shall command the blessing upon thee in thy storehouses, and in all that thou settest thine hand unto; and he shall bless thee in the land which the LORD thy God giveth thee" *(Deuteronomy 28:8).*

Therefore, as I engage in any business this year, it shall be a profitable investment. Businesses shall become too easy for me this year. My storehouses shall be filled with divine blessings.

For it is also written,

"The LORD shall establish thee an holy people unto himself, as he hath sworn unto thee, if thou shalt keep the commandments of the LORD thy God, and walk in his ways" (Deuteronomy 28:9).

Therefore, I bind the spirit of failure and demons laboring to destroy my life's investments. I paralyze the root of vagabond spirit that is moving me from place to place without a definite establishment. In the name of Jesus, I begin to establish my ministry and every good thing to the glory of God. O Lord, please do not allow me to destroy what you have built in me. I shall be established forever and ever. I command every spirit of destruction to any investment to vanish forever in my life. O Lord, invest Your nature and Your authority in my life. Let the fruits and gifts of the Spirit be invested in my life, in the name of Jesus. Amen.

Decree For Settlement

The power in the name of Jesus is settling me today, in the name of Jesus. I shall be settled this year martially and financially. The blood of Jesus will not allow me to be moved back and forth by Satan. This year, whether devil likes it or not, I shall be settled in all areas of my life. I receive the power to be settled by the blood of the lamb.

For it is written, "The LORD shall establish thee an holy people unto himself, as he hath sworn unto thee, if thou shalt keep the commandments of the LORD thy God, and walk in his ways. And all people of the earth shall see that thou art called by the name of the LORD; and they shall be afraid of thee. And the LORD shall make thee plenteous in goods, in the fruit of thy body, and in the fruit of thy cattle, and in the fruit of thy ground, in the land which the LORD swore unto thy fathers to give thee" (Deuteronomy 28:9-11).

Therefore, as I walk in God's ways this year, I shall be settled in the perfect will of God. I shall be settled by the Lord in plenty of goods and in all aspects of life. Any power fighting against my settlement shall die. Let all strangers in my promise land die by fire immediately. Any strange man or woman sitting on my position, be unseated by force. Anger of God, break the backbone of the spirit of poverty in my life. Blood of Jesus, carry my destiny across the Red Sea.

Any evil blockade to my divine settlement in life, be removed by fire and force, in the name of Jesus. I reject any counterfeit settlement that is about to take place in my life. I shall meet with people that will settle me the way God has planned it. O Lord, my God, begin to settle me by fire, in the name of Jesus.

Decree For Favor

I decree divine favor to possess me wherever I am now. Blood of Jesus, speak favor into my life. I surrender completely to favor to take over me immediately.

For it is written,

"When a man's ways please the LORD, he maketh even his enemies to be at peace with him" (Proverbs 16:7).

O Lord, let me please You effortlessly without pain. Let even my enemies begin to favor me. Blood of Jesus, put the banner of favor upon me now and forever. Divine and unmerited favors, wherever you are, catch me and overwhelm me by fire. O Lord, soak me in Your favor forever and ever. Anointing of favor, possess me and manipulate me to the glory of God. Fire of favor, burn all over my body and destroy disfavor spirits in my life. In all the days of my life, I will know the favor of the LORD.

For it is written,

"And not only they, but ourselves also, which have the firstfruits of the Spirit, even we ourselves groan within ourselves, waiting for the adoption, to wit, the redemption of our body" (Romans 8:23).

Therefore, by the power in the Word of God, I receive abundant favor now. No good thing will the Lord withhold from me henceforth. You my enemies and friends, you must favor me. Revival for divine favor, possess me. I decree death to the spirit of disfavor in my life, in the name of Jesus. Bread of afflictions, pursue every demons causing disfavor in my life, in the name of Jesus. I command death to every sin that is stealing favors from my destiny.

Let there be bitter destruction upon witchcraft spirits fighting against the favor of God in my life. O Lord, take me to the city of favor and breakthrough, in the name of Jesus, Amen.

Decree For Journey Mercy

O Lord, I thank You for all powers belong to You. It is written, "O thou that hearest prayer, unto thee shall all flesh come" (Psalms 65:2).

O Lord, hear my prayers this hour and grant me journey mercies. There shall be no accident, death, and locomotive problems. Everything about this journey shall be perfected to the glory of God. The blood of Jesus will go before us and behind us. We shall go in peace and return in peace.

For it is written,

"No weapon that is formed against thee shall prosper; and every tongue that shall rise against thee in judgment thou shalt condemn. This is the heritage of the servants of the LORD, and their righteousness is of me, saith the LORD" (Isaiah 54:17).

Therefore, any weapon formed against us in this journey shall not prosper, it shall backfire. Every tongue that shall rise against this traveling shall be condemned, I shall not die. This journey will be filled with testimonies. The eaters of flesh and drinkers of blood shall drink their own blood and eat their own flesh. The eyes of evil ones shall not see us as we make this journey. Powers of evil ones shall be incapacitated for the sake of this journey, in the name of Jesus.

O Lord, grant me traveling mercies now, to the end. Let divine whirlwind take away every evil blockade along this journey. Horrible tempest, carry away evil messengers in this journey, in the name of Jesus. I stand against every form of confusion in this journey and I release death upon spirits of confusion and death, in the name of Jesus, Amen.

Decree For Your Birthday

O Lord, thank You for adding another year to my years. I will ever remain grateful to You, O Lord, in this life and in the life after. Now, let every demon that is opposing the hand of God in my life be wasted. O Lord, give me a birthday gift that will honor Your name. I shall not die a premature death; my years and youth shall be renewed.

For it is written,

"The days of our years are threescore years and ten; and if by reason of strength they be fourscore years, yet is their strength labor and sorrow; for it is soon cut off, and we fly away" (Psalms 90:10).

Therefore, I shall not die young. O Lord, keep me as young as ever and help me to please You in all the days of my life. My enemies shall not cut my life short. The champions of the Philistines shall not kill me. I shall kill my Goliath. All Egyptian armies that are pursuing me shall perish in the

Red Sea. I shall reach my promise land immediately. My Joseph shall not die in prison.

From today, I escape from every evil prison yard to the palace of King Jesus. O Lord, renew my years and give me the grace to walk with You until I walked into heaven like Enoch. If I will die at all, let it be like Elijah, David or by the rapture of the saints.

For it is written,

"For David, after he had served his own generation by the will of God, fell on sleep, and was laid unto his fathers, and saw corruption" (Acts 13:36).

I receive the grace to serve my generation by the will of God, in the name of Jesus. No power shall kill or destroy me until I fulfill my ministry and destiny.

Decree Against Any Form Of Haman

I decree that spiritually, Haman shall die in my place. He will die on his own gallows. Before Herod will see me, I shall escape, in the name of Jesus. Herod would die while I still live.

For it is written,

"But when Herod was dead, behold, an angel of the Lord appeareth in a dream to Joseph in Egypt, Saying, Arise, and take the young child and his mother, and go into the land of Israel: for they are dead which sought the young child's life. And he arose, and took the young child and his mother, and came into the land of Israel. But when he heard that Archelaus did reign in Judaea in the room of his father Herod, he was afraid to go thither: notwithstanding, being warned of God in a dream, he turned aside into the parts of Galilee" (Matthew 2:19-23).

Therefore, I decree death to Herod and I claim perfect healing by fire. Although John was beheaded, I shall not submit to the sword of the enemy, in the name of Jesus.

For it is written,

"And the children of Israel went into the midst of the sea upon the dry ground: and the waters were a wall unto them on their right hand, and on their left. And the Egyptians pursued, and went in after them to the midst of the sea, even all Pharaoh's horses, his chariots, and his horsemen. And it came to pass, that in the morning watch the LORD looked unto the host of the Egyptians through the pillar of fire and of the cloud, and troubled the host of the Egyptians, And took off their chariot wheels, that they drave them heavily: so that the Egyptians said, Let us flee from the face of Israel; for the LORD fighteth for them against the Egyptians. And the LORD said unto Moses, Stretch out thine hand over the sea, that the waters may come again upon the Egyptians, upon their chariots, and upon their

horsemen. And Moses stretched forth his hand over the sea, and the sea returned to his strength when the morning appeared; and the Egyptians fled against it; and the LORD overthrew the Egyptians in the midst of the sea. And the waters returned, and covered the chariots, and the horsemen, and all the host of Pharaoh that came into the sea after them; there remained not so much as one of them. But the children of Israel walked upon dry land in the midst of the sea; and the waters were a wall unto them on their right hand, and on their left. Thus the LORD saved Israel that day out of the hand of the Egyptians; and Israel saw the Egyptians dead upon the seashore. And Israel saw that great work which the LORD did upon the Egyptians: and the people feared the LORD, and believed the LORD, and his servant Moses" (Exodus 14:22-31).

Therefore, let all the host of Egyptians armies that are pursuing after my life be overthrown by the Lord, in the name of Jesus. Let all the old prophets that are coming after my life die while I live to fulfill my ministry.

For it is written,

> *"And as the king of Israel was passing by upon the wall, there cried a woman unto him, saying, Help, my lord, O king. And he said, if the LORD do not help thee, whence shall I help thee? Out of the barn floor, or out of the winepress? And the king said unto her, what aileth thee? And she answered, this woman said unto me, give thy son that we may eat him to day, and we will eat my son tomorrow. So we boiled my son, and did eat him: and I said unto her on the next day, Give thy son, that we may eat him: and she hath hid her son" (2 Kings 6:26-29).*

I decree that my case is different; therefore, any witch or wizard that wants to boil me alive shall die first. O Lord, if You must kill, kill, and if You must destroy, destroy so that I can live longer than Haman and Herod spiritually.

For it is written,

"And Harbonah, one of the chamberlains, said before the king, Behold also, the gallows fifty cubits high, which Haman had made for Mordecai, who had spoken good for the king, standeth in the house of Haman. Then the king said, Hang him thereon. So they hanged Haman on the gallows that he had prepared for Mordecai. Then was the king's wrath pacified" (Esther 7:9-10).

Therefore, by the decree of the Lord, I command all Haman to be hanged on their own gallows, in the name of Jesus, Amen.

THANK YOU!

I'd like to use this time to thank you for purchasing my books and helping my ministry and work. Any copy of my book you buy helps to fund my ministry and family, as well as offering much-needed inspiration to keep writing. My family and I are very thankful, and we take your assistance very seriously.

You have already accomplished so much, but I would appreciate an honest review of some of my books through the link below. This is critical since reviews reflect how much an author's work is respected.

Please [click here] to leave a review on Amazon. If you're viewing from a printed version, please visit amazon.com/review/create-review?asin=1466244100 to leave a review.

Please be aware that I read and value all comments and reviews. You can always post a review even though you haven't finished the book yet, and then edit your reviews later.

Thank you so much as you spare a precious moment of your time and may God bless you and meet you at the very point of your need.

You can also send me an email to hello@madueke.com if you encounter any difficulty while writing your review.

PRAYER M. MADUEKE'S BESTSELLING BOOKS

Click on any of the [Buy Now] buttons to view or purchase them on my website. If you're viewing from a printed version, please visit madueke.com and search for these books.

1. Dictionary of Demons & Complete Deliverance — [Buy Now]

2. Monitoring Spirits — [Buy Now]

3. Praying with The Blood of Jesus — [Buy Now]

4. The Power of Speaking in Tongues — [Buy Now]

5. Speaking Things into Existence by Faith — [Buy Now]

6. Discerning and Defeating the Ahab & Jezebel Spirit — [Buy Now]

7. Defeating the Python Spirit — [Buy Now]

8. 35 Special Dangerous Decrees — [Buy Now]

9. 21/40 Nights of Decrees and Your Enemies Will Surrender — [Buy Now]

10. Command the Morning, Day and Night   [Buy Now]

11. Evil Summon   [Buy Now]

12. Overcoming & Destroying the Spirit of
    Rejection & Hatred   [Buy Now]

13. Queen of Heaven: Wife of Satan   [Buy Now]

14. The False Prophet   [Buy Now]

15. Dominion Over Sickness & Disease   [Buy Now]

16. The Battle Plan for Destroying
    Foundational Witchcraft   [Buy Now]

17. The Queen of the Coast   [Buy Now]

18. Dictionary of Unmerited Favor   [Buy Now]

19. Prayers for Breakthrough in your Business   [Buy Now]

20. A Jump From Evil Altar   [Buy Now]

21. 100 Days Prayers to Wake Up Your
    Lazarus   [Buy Now]

22. Breaking Evil Yokes   [Buy Now]

23. When Evil Altars are Multiplied   [Buy Now]

24. The Battle Plan for Destroying
    Foundational Occultism   [**Buy Now**]

25. Prayers for Protection   [**Buy Now**]

26. Prayers for Academic Success   [**Buy Now**]

27. Your Dream Directory   [**Buy Now**]

28. Prayers for Financial Breakthrough   [**Buy Now**]

29. Destiny and Star Hunters   [**Buy Now**]

30. Prayers to Pray during Courtship   [**Buy Now**]

31. 91 Days Decrees to Takeover the Year   [**Buy Now**]

32. Alone with God   [**Buy Now**]

33. Prayers against Satanic Oppression   [**Buy Now**]

34. Foundations Exposed   [**Buy Now**]

35. Prayers for Deliverance   [**Buy Now**]

36. Prayers to Heal Broken Relationship   [**Buy Now**]

37. Prayers for Good Health   [**Buy Now**]

4 Free Ebooks

In order to say a 'Thank You' for purchasing *35 Special Dangerous Decrees*, I offer these books to you in appreciation. Click or type madueke.com/free-gift in your browser.

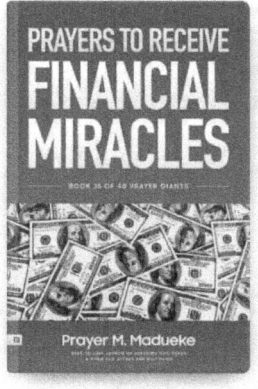

Video Bonus

I've created exclusive video content to complement the topics covered in the book. These videos provide deeper insights and discussions on the things discussed in this book, offering you a more immersive learning experience.

To access the video bonus for this course, simply click or type links.madueke.com/12SDD in your browser.

Message from the Author

I want to see you succeed, grow, and break free from negativity and obstacles. My hope is for you to thrive, unaffected by negative influences and challenging situations. Because of that, please permit me to introduce two courses that I believe passionately will help you:

1. To break the evil altars and powers of your father's house, The role of altars in the realm of existence is very key because altars are meeting places between the physical and the spiritual, between the visible and the invisible.

    Unless a man cuts off the evil flow from the power of his father's house, he will not fulfil his destiny. Click here to learn more about my course on how to tear down unholy altars and close the enemy's entryways into your life!

2. To help you seamlessly break iron-like problems, illness, delayed marriage, poverty, or any long-standing battle.

    Discover the transformative power of Christian fasting and prayer. Remember, Matthew 17:21 teaches us, *"But this kind of demon does not go out except by prayer and fasting."* Ready to overcome your struggles? Click here to learn more about this course.

Embrace the journey ahead with faith, for through prayer, fasting, and the dismantling of evil altars, you shall unlock the doors to spiritual liberation and divine breakthrough. May your path be illuminated by His grace as you walk towards a life free from bondage.

If you're seeing this from the physical copy, type the link: madueke.com/courses in your browser to view all the courses on my website.

Prayer Madueke
CHRISTIAN AUTHOR

Christian Counselling

We were created for a greater purpose than only survival and God wants us to live a full life.

If you need prayer or counselling, or if you have any other inquiries, please visit the counselling page on my website to know when I will be available for a phone call.

Click or type **links.madueke.com/counselling** in your browser.

Let's Connect on Youtube ▶️

Join me on my YouTube channel, "Prayer M. Madueke," where I share powerful insights, guidance, and prayers for spiritual breakthroughs.

Subscribe today to unlock the secrets of the Kingdom and embrace an abundant life. Let's grow together!

Click or type links.madueke.com/youtube in your browser.

An Invitation to Become a Ministry Partner

I appreciate the support and inquiries I have received regarding collaboration with my ministry. Your prayers and dedication to the work of the Kingdom are highly valued.

You can also visit the donation page on my website if you would like to contribute or learn more about supporting my ministry: madueke.com/donate.

Thank you for your continued support and faithfulness in Christ Jesus.